MEXICAN
MURAL
PAINTING

MURAL PAINTING OF THE MEXICAN REVOLUTION

FONDO DE CULTURA ECONÓMICA — MÉXICO

FIRST EDITION IN SPANISH AND ENGLISH, 1960. SECOND EDITION IN ENGLISH, 1967. PRODUCED BY ARTIA FOR THE FONDO DE CULTURA ECONÓMICA (AV. DE LA UNIVERSIDAD, 975) MÉXICO 12, D.F.
 - PRINTED AND MADE IN CZECHOSLOVAKIA.

CONTENTS

INTRODUCTION

IN MEXICO, AS IN THE ENTIRE WORLD, ART HAS BEEN THE CONSEQUENCE OF man's spiritual energy.

In war or peace, night or day, the human being as a condense of unique conditions has achieved through art the remarkable feat of giving permanence to the passing moment. The artist has made the past permanently present. He has captured time, sensation and emotion–thanks to memory, which receives and conserves what we see and hear, what our hands touch, what we taste, indifferent to whether it be good or evil. The work of art is time solidified in emotions and sensations, which are thus isolated by an apparently inexplicable necessity.

The artist communicates 'something' to us that we need. Herein lies the social value of art, and its concomitant force and firm solidarity with all spiritual values. The end-purpose of human conduct is to give form to some entity.

Beauty is all that which gives us pleasure, even in spite of ourselves. It is an order of always different things, fruit of the artist's creative energy. If the work of art is the declaration of a consummated act, its consequence is criticism or the opinion it arouses in each one of us. 'I like it' or 'I don't like it' is the affinity measure or relation we all have to the created art work. We like things on finding some part of ourselves in them, or vice versa. Either attraction or difference, and the difference is in essence an attraction, too.

Art is the universal language which convinces us of human unity. What impedes man from living poetically is selfishness, and the unconfessed drive to self-love, so inhuman and absurd.

The value of art is unique among norms of human interchange. It furnishes us a supreme reality of matter, in differing versions, according to the capacity of the artist. The world is architectonic and sculptural, it has color, music, poetry. We know this when the artist states it to us. And through art, our perceptions are verified so surely that our feeling of admiration, entering into combination with poetic reality, spontaneously flourishes. It is as if we have made a discovery.

In Mexico's geographical area, man has demonstrated his artistic capacity. From north to south, from Zacatecas to Chiapas, in the highlands and in the lowlands, in the tropics, everywhere there was gigantic art activity. Examples of superlative richness and variety everywhere accumulated, showing the creative genius of our indigenous world. This ancient people organized vast cultural cycles that recount in stone, in clay, in stucco, on painted walls and on paper, adventures of the body and mind whether in religion or daily life.

Men and influences came from all directions, spilling into the cornucopia of Mexico and left an inheritance of life and survivals that are an invitation to universality. Were the La Venta sculptors Negroid? From what Oriental region did the primitive Mayas come? And the architects of Teotihuacan? The last act of the indigenous drama ends tragically. Art transmuted into a heroic life — it was Cuauhtémoc's! Over the corpse of an entire people, Europe marched. It brought us, artistically speaking, its accumulation from the young Greek world, the Roman, the Gothic, and finally its contemporary Renaissance culture — an Italian resumé of the three fore-mentioned cultures, which Italy's enthusiastic spirit prodigiously rejuvenated. But this Europe was Spain, and brought, too, Moorish accents. Then at the close of the XVI Century, a new Oriental wave reached Acapulco.

And our ancient geographical cornucopia — between the European sword and the Oriental wall — was filled with undecipherable inscriptions and a new language and a new idea of God.

But the Indian, though mistreated unto sorrow, hid his vivid ingenuity and his neverending imagination, only expressing it in crafts and at times in higher arts. The baroque arrived. Mexico assimilated it with super-abundant energy and expressed it with independence–showing that Mexico could be free as it once was, and again would be. The Christian altars of the XVII Century are complicated oratories of gold and archangels. The Indian hand was resolving problems, sometimes difficult ones, and let itself go to create those delicious marvels of the Tonantzintla and Tlacochahuaya churches.

Neoclassic style at the end of the XVIII and beginning of the XIX centuries was, from the artistic point of view, a very false religious expression. Mexico accepted it, and in order to follow it, destroyed works of art in which the Mexican element had emerged in affinity and delight. A trip to some parts of Puebla and Tlaxcala states shows us, in both civil and religious architecture, Oriental reminiscences in external decoration with glazed ceramic. In the Bajio, pear-shaped cupolas in yellow or white give cities and countryside a special touch, and are the result of Neoclassic style.

A few years after the Reform, a landscapist, a portrait artist and an engraver in their work heralded the reappearance of Mexico in the art world.

Velasco painted the Valley of Mexico at his highest horizons, giving cosmic value to his painting.

Hermenegildo Bustos was an extraordinary portrait painter, combining profound insight into the model with technical vigor.

And as for Posada, his black and white scripted the whole history of an era whose plastic chronicler he was.

The Revolution is born. The Díaz government dies. Madero comes, but his betrayal by Huerta, too. These three years were Posada's last in life the inspiring flames of the great Mexican mural painting. Diego Rivera, José Clemente Orozco and David Alfaro Siqueiros, lifted this mural movement.

ANTECEDENTS

THE PRE-HISPANIC PERIOD

UP TO OUR DAY, INVESTIGATIONS CONTINUE AS TO WHETHER THE PRIMITIVE inhabitants of the Americas did not originate here. It is claimed they came over the Bering Strait and that perhaps other groups, following maritime currents, reached the Americas from Polynesia. Our indigenes resemble the Mongolian type physically.

From twelve to fourteen thousand years ago, man hunted elephants and horses in the Valley of Mexico. Later, when he invented agriculture, he became sedentary, acquired set customs. The man was forced to protect himself against the climate and he also had to satisfy his daily life needs; he could achieve this only by improving his shelter and his utensils of immediate use. At first he drank kneeling at the waters, then from the cup of his hand, and this gave him the idea of a recipient — and so ceramics originated. Then he thought of adding a handle to facilitate holding the bowl. And from utility he advanced to beauty, when he decorated the clay. He moved from the cave to the hut, and from the hut to the room-divided house.

Creation itself suggested the idea of God to him. Natural forces–earth and water, air and fire–were for him a motif of adoration. The change of seasons indicated to him the notion of time, and interchange between families resulted in social living and the origin of government. If the gods presided over and dominated all, their tangible representation had to be set higher than the houses of man. Thus was originated the construction of pyramids on which temples were built. Pyramidal construction is the principal characteristic of religious architecture in the territory of Mexico before the Conquest.

To the south of Mexico's capital a conical construction emerges on the plain of gigantic lava waves, petrified for more than three thousand years. It is more than fifteen meters high and its ascent is a spiral ramp. Cuicuilco is probably the oldest example of our architecture.

The Americas' basic food has always been corn, just as rice is in China and India, wheat in the Middle East. Whether corn originated in Mexico or Peru is a subject of discussion. *Metates* or stone artifacts used to grind corn have been found beneath the layer of lava which ruined Copilco and Cuicuilco. Man sows at the approach of the rainy season. Earth receives the seed in her depths, and aided by humidity, produces the nourishing grain. When man dies, he is buried and becomes dust. Thus, the earth is mother and grave. It nourishes the human with vital substances and receives back into its depths the sower himself. We breathe air, we drink water, we cultivate the earth, we use fire. Among these four elemental forces, man has his existence. His power of will is the basis of all his activity. His natural and heroic impulse, for his own well-being, is to dominate the elements and obtain better production with less effort.

Man's struggle and progress in a world of matter have brought him during some thousands of years since the invention of the door, to the placement of an artifact on the Moon. All progress in dominating matter has been made, if comparing it with brief human life, in a long time scheme; but if comparing it with man's history, in a short time lapse. To the primitive, the four elements of matter merited adoration — for his benefit and in his fear. The Sun was the supreme deity, and the

Moon and stars were a motive of veneration as well. The Sun, source and origin of all energy. The Moon, influencing all animal and vegetable life. The idea of good and evil determined moral values, and with religious feeling the idea of immortality became concrete. Osiris, in Egypt, seemed only a symbol. The Greeks personified the symbols, and made all divine. In India, twenty-six centuries ago, Buddha, a young prince, sat calm and motionless under a fig tree, his legs crossed, and preached that by sacrificing desire man achieves perfection.

Two thousand years ago, a young worker traveled actively through cities and towns of Palestine and with outstretched arms gave Humanity this exhortation: 'Love one another.' His doctrine of love is based on forgiveness which with the abolition of hate and condemnation of accumulated wealth, offers the possibility of fraternity — whose joy gives hope of immortal life. Quetzalcoatl, luminous shadow, passes over the spiritual horizon of ancient Mexico, and becoming divine, transforming himself into a heavenly star accompanies the Sun in its birth and death, in a legend that seems story but expresses deep human emotion.

Art as religious expression has reached most surprising developments. Almost all of the ancient art of Mexico, as nearly everywhere else, is certainly religious in character.

In each artistic cycle we observe three periods: the formative, the apogee and the decadent; that is, the pre-classic, the classic and the post-classic. In the first millenium before Christ, culture in Mexico was formalized. If the primitive inhabitants came from Asia, was their culture born here or did they bring it with them? Scientific investigation continues seeking clarification of this unknown.

In that first millenium B.C., a culture evolved and extended not only throughout almost all our national territory but also to almost the entire Americas. We call it the Olmec or La Venta culture. The locale corresponds to present-day Tabasco state, where the most notable ceremonial center is found. The Olmecs were primordially sculptors: colossal heads, altars, stelae, animal sculptures, obelisks. Some of these sculptures, of gigantic size, some of them weighing more than thirty tons, reveal artistic genius based on reality, fruit of maturity and impassioned labor. A magnificent sense of the monumental prevails in all of this culture's art. It left, too, jade carvings of singular mastery. Some archeologists hold that the La Venta culture gave origin to all, or almost all, the pre-Hispanic cultures of Mexico; or that it at least influenced the development of some of them. Already in this culture we find elevated earth constructions and pyramidal earth platforms. Were these men perhaps the initiators of the sciences related to the calendar?

About 500 years B.C., north west of Mexico City at a site called Tlatilco, ceramics flourished. In tombs there were found bowls of fine form and feminine figurines of rare beauty.

Around the first centuries of our era, still in the Valley of Mexico, our greatest architectonic work appears: the ceremonial center of Teotihuacan-pyramids and courts, temples and palaces, all richly decorated. The magnificent ruins reveal the genius of the builders who achieved masterpieces in all the arts. Teotihuacan art is characterized by virile force and austere elegance. Whether we view the Sun pyramid–seventy meters high and two hundred wide — or either we fix our sight on a jar painted *al fresco*, our admiration is one and the same.

A hundred kilometers north of Teotihuacan, in the X Century, a new culture center named Tollan (Tula), arises. Product of the Toltec civilization, it has vivid Teotihuacan influences. Thus to some extent the Toltec is a sequence of the Teotihuacan, just as the Aztec — insofar as culture is concerned — is a sequence of the Toltec. Twenty-five centuries of culture, counting from the year 1000 B.C. to 1521 A.D. when the invasion and domination by Europeans were to change so profoundly the cultural organization of the ancient peoples of the American Continent.

The pyramid was the common denominator of pre-Hispanic religious architecture. In Tula the Toltecs, too, built them and above all gave to sculpture novel use as a supplement to architecture. Examples are: the relief panels used on façades of buildings; the transformation of the human figure into columns, and the design of extraordinary serpent columns, all these pillars being used to sustain temple roofs (Tula and Chichen Itza). Tula was destroyed by semi-barbarous tribes at the middle of the XII Century, and soon the Toltecs appeared in Yucatan with such impact that, blending their culture with the Maya, they left in Chichen Itza the most grandiose expression of their artistic genius. It is only through these art manifestations that we know the cultural explosion emanating from Mexico's center to its south and southeast. Before the Toltecs went to Yucatan, the Teotihuacan culture had vigorously influenced the Zapotecs (Oaxaca), as shown by their architecture (Monte Alban) and painting (first centuries of our era).

In the great ceremonial center of Monte Alban, we find that the pre-Zapotec is prescient of Olmec culture. Not until its ceramic of the classic epoch and its final architectonic phase did the purely Zapotec appear with unmistakable accent. The funeral urns of Monte Alban and the incomparable structures at Mitla are examples.

At Monte Alban, architecture has the majestic sobriety of the Teotihuacan culture. Ceramic sculpture, on the contrary, is ornamentally complex and stunning in inventive richness. Mitla, 50 kilometers east of Monte Alban, in the luminous Oaxaca Valley, is one of the most beautiful architectonic masses in the world. The region is subject to frequent earthquakes, and has sparse plant life; the plastic cacti of differing kinds and notable patterns seem to defend a strangely-mystic land with their spines and thorns. Due to the zone's tendency to earthquakes, the architects preferred low, long, horizontal structure. The stone material, marvelously sculpted, at times astounds us by the size of its blocks. The decoration by inserted plaques seems a geometric discourse in the language of Greek frets, wherein rhythmic beauty imparts a prodigious sonority. Nowhere in the world is there anything like these structures, full of measured poetry in the rhetoric of landscape whose light appears to be created as their background. Referring to the Mixtecs, another people of the Oaxaca region, their legacy among other values is a brilliantly-painted ceramic and, of highest importance, the codices or books referring to their religion and dynasties–true masterworks for beauty and original painting.

The Totonac culture flourished in what today is the state of Veracruz, and had in its origins a marked Olmec, or La Venta, influence. The Totonac classic phase is characterized by pyramid constructions in sections of niches. The Tajin ceremonial center, near Papantla, is justly famous. Totonac art produced the very handsome stone carvings called *yugos*, *hachas*, and *palmas*. In clay sculpture, the Totonacs reached heights of emotional expression through this medium that few artists have attained in universal art. Seldom has any people laughed so happily, and transmitted this laughter so admirably, as the Totonacs in their sculpture.

The Mayan civilization is the most complete and perfect of all the cultural cycles in ancient Mexo-America and Central America. Before the Christian era, Olmec inheritance entered into Mayan origins. The Mayas occupied the entire southeast area of Mexico, as well as what are today

Belice, Guatemala and Honduras. Their importance is as great in science as in art. They invented the zero and positional mathematics. Their astronomical observations amaze us. Their time computation on the earth's movement around the sun is the most precise up to the modern day. And only about a third of their hieroglyphic writing has been deciphered. Of their literature, there remains to us that most extraordinary work, the *Popol-Vuh*, a splendid poetic interpretation of the marvelous creation of the universe and the origins of Humanity.

Mayan art, a stupendous tropical harvest, is characterized by its profound elegance and by realistic representation of the human figure as beauty. The Mayan moment is a zenith of history, inspiring love of mankind and deep-felt respect for man. Uxmal, Sayil, Tulum, Chinkultik and Labna — a geography of rhythm. The Mayan cities have immortal Mayan names. In architecture, their arch, triangular in shape due to its mass, limited the space covered but in many instances resisted the rain-forest, that implacable enemy of this great tropical culture. Palenque is, without doubt, the supreme expression of Mayan genius. Eight centuries ago, after the fall of Tula, the Toltecs mysteriously traveled to Yucatan, and the contact of the two cultures gave Chichen-Itza enormous stature. Nowhere in ancient America do we find two cultures so admirably interlaced. Ten years ago when the mural paintings of Bonampak (Chiapas) were discovered, we were astounded anew at the artistic genius of the Mayas. We saw with surprise, too, the affinity of these paintings with Diego Rivera's murals, done years before the discovery of these VIII Century painting. To sum up, the Mayan civilization was all-embracing.

When the Europeans invaded Mexico at the beginning of the XVI Century and destroyed the indigene civilization, it had been two hundred years that a Nahua group, after many difficulties, gained foothold in the Valley of Mexico. On the salt lake they had been relegated to an inhospitable island where they built their huts that a century and a half later were to become 'an immense stone flower'. At the close of the XV Century, Tenoxtitlan was one of the principal cities of the world. Its founders had overcome all obstacles and unleashed their drives, forming a military caste first for defense and later for domination, and had warred as far as Central America where the Nahuatl language today still exists in many place names. From the Toltecs they learned science and art.

The singular and awesome rite of this warlike Nahua people was blood sacrifice said to nourish the Sun. In strange contrast, they adored flowers with poetic devotion. In their calendar of twenty-day months, one day each month was dedicated to death, and equally, one day a month, to a flower.

In the second half of the XV Century, Aztec sculptors were marvelous. No other people ever worked so many tons of stone in so few years. Basalt and diorite yielded to chisels made of harder rock and from gigantic slabs emerged the astounding forms of the earth goddess, Coatlicue, with her serpent-woven skirts, and of the Sun image, surrounded by four preceding suns and the plastic rendering of the days. The first of these sculptures is one of the most grandiose concepts man ever formulated. The subject is the earth, and its adjectives are earth's symbolic attributes. Man's heart, his hands, his skull — successively earth's son, its master and its victim. In this stupendous synthesis, words fail and stone speaks. Being and time are the minor angles of the Nahua metaphorical pyramid, and its vertex is immortal death. One of the most extraordinary relics at our great museum is time's tomb. It is a small construction, of about one cubic meter, made from worked pieces of volcanic lava, decorated with skulls and crossed bones. In the interior, the bonds of time, as it were, are seen in the form of clusters of twigs tied at each end, all simulated in stone. They are the records of perished time, sepulchrally preserved. Time cadaverized time now dead. Nothing like it exists in the history of universal culture.

In recent years, at the tip of everybody's tongue are Aztec poetic fragments translated from manuscripts written in Nahuatl and set down in European letter. The remarkable cleric Garibay started an ample course of investigation into the intellectual life of this people. As translator as well as investigator, he has reached outstanding transcendence in the integration of the Mexican spirit.

More than four and a half centuries later, the Mexican of the highlands remains true to remote tradition. In the first days of November, people make sugar-candy skulls and 'bread of the dead'. We eat death. Toys made for these days also have a funeral note.

Near the vestiges of the razed imperial city, skulls still appear as in ancient times. In an angle of the cathedral's courtyard, at the foot of the crosses, eight white, stone skulls remind us that nearby was the *tzompantli*, a wooden tower where hung the skulls of those sacrificed so that their blood would nourish the Sun. It is a moving coincidence that sculpturally prolongs the visual tradition of familiarity with death.

The Americas' invasion and conquest by Europeans took place in the first third of the XVI Century. The Renaissance was then reaching maturity. Its art, reacting against the Gothic of the late Middle Ages, was inspired by Graeco-Roman ideas. Along these lines the mestization of Ibero-America was led almost to our times. Unless something resembled the Graeco-Latin or Renaissance, it was not considered lovely artistic. In the last thirty years, a taste and love for pre-Hispanic art have been born in such a vital way that where formerly its investigation and study were carried out by foreigners, now our own pursue this field enthusiastically. However, foreigners have not ceased to be passionately interested in these matters. Mexico and Peru have enriched Europe and the U.S. in current years with great pre-Hispanic art collections sent to them on exhibition tours and arousing the greatest admiration. The Americas' ancient art is as important as that of Egypt, Greece, China. But our art must be seen, with all its unique originality, just as Greek or Egyptian art, to be appreciated. No, the Europeans did not bring us culture. They brought us *their* culture. Civilization, art and science existed in our Americas long before they did in Europe.

Art can be realist or it can be conventional, or it may partake of both categories. It is impossible to equal Nature. But Nature can be rivalled. The acceptable and admirable realist criterion is to infuse it with the poetry that exists in us. Conventionalism consists of representing nature not as it is, but as we would like it to be. Frequently, the ceramic sculpture of West Mexico is more conventional than realist. The Mayas delighted in a sensual art accepting the sheer loveliness of the human body (Palenque and Piedras Negras). Mixtec codex paintings are conventional and of fascinating beauty. Mexican archeology is one of the most outstanding and doubtless the most varied that any country in the world can offer.

The name 'Mexico' derives from the word *Mexi* and the end syllable *co* which indicates place. Mexico: place of *Mexi*, the high priest who finally settled the Nahua group of founders at the site of Tenoxtitlan. Thus we speak of Aztec culture, or better still, *Mexica* culture. Therefore, Mexican . . .

Mexico's ancient art is the chief root of our Mexican being. Knowing it, loving it, admiring it, we integrate fully. It is being — on splendid scale.

THE COLONIAL DOMINATION

IN THE OPEN AIR, AT THE SOUTH CORNER OF THE MEXICO CITY CATHEDRAL, there are some sculpted stones carefully left there. They are testimony in rock to one of the greatest moments in our history. These fragments are from the principal temple of the ancient Mexica capital, and we see in them on one hand, indigene work, and on the other, European style undoubtedly produced by the indigene hand. These fragments of columns belonged to the first Mexico City cathedral, constructed within the perimeter of ancient Tenoxtitlan's main square. Later, and on the same site, at the close of the same XVI Century, the sovereign cathedral which we now admire was constructed. Thus artistic continuity was a fact by virtue of religious sentiment.

The Spanish conquest destroyed the two latest pre-Hispanic cultures in the Americas, for no reason whatsoever: the Mexica or Aztec culture of Mexico, and the Inca culture of Peru. The former masters of these civilizations were reduced to servitude. The conquest was as brutal as any other in the world, and left the two peoples so deeply wounded that even today, after more than four centuries, the pariah state of our aborigines — their alienation from society — saddens us as our greatest misfortune.

Christian missionaries, of whom some were eminent for their kindness and wisdom, partly sweetened the lot of the enslaved peoples and saved from complete oblivion a good portion of the information relating those peoples' culture and civilization. The missionaries taught a doctrine that, miraculously, was accepted and sustained in an environment of Spanish example completely contradictory to Christianity — wherever there were Spanish civil and military authorities, and that was everywhere. Among the missionaries were men outstanding for their interest in, and intelligence about the cultures destroyed by violence and greed. Bernardino de Sahagún, the Franciscan monk, became the father of our ancient history by writing his monumental *Historia de las cosas de Nueva España* (History of the Things of New Spain) in the middle of the XVI Century. Another historian-monk, Bartolomé de las Casas, was the most tenacious and courageous defender of the Indians. The monk Toribio de Benavente (Motolinía), historian and educator like Sahagún, a mirror of humility, activity and cheerfulness, planned and founded in the XVIII Century the city of Puebla de los Angeles, one of the most beautiful cities of the Americas. The missionaries were also the builders of the new churches which during the XVI Century served as storehouses and fortresses. Churches and convents multiplied and frequently were built on sacred ancient sites and with materials taken from the demolished temples.

The city of Tenoxtitlan fell in August, 1521, martyred by a siege of almost three months. With the city fell its defender, young Cuauhtémoc, whose fire-tortured feet walk forever toward glory. He left us his great example of heroism and of love for independence and liberty. Cuauhtémoc is the ideal hero-type everywhere and for all times. His hangman, Hernán Cortés, died in 1547 at about which time the first important construction of churches and convents began.

These first buildings at times revive three European styles: the Roman, the Gothic and the Renaissance; as if their architects dedicated themselves to the transplanting of Christian architecture on the Americas' soil. The end dome, above the main altar, is actually sustained by filaments of Gothic characteristics. The façade reveals the florid elegance of the Renaissance, and the cloisters are upheld by Roman-style arches and columns, the first truly Christian style (X to XIII centuries). The most beautiful constructions of this period are at Actopan, Acolman and Yuririapundaro. At times at the angles of the great courtyards, they built small adoratories used for special celebrations. In Calpan, Puebla state, these are outstanding for their marvelous sculptures. Mural painting, generally in white and black, had great prominence as we can see principally at Actopan and Acolman. At Epazoyuca color was used. The painted figures at Acolman have a curious resemblance to Michelangelo in style and size. The indigene was not only a mason but a sculptor as well. The missionaries always allowed him a margin of expression, and often a line, a flower, a cherub, is an inheritance of ancient Mexican sculpture. Moorish-influenced elements entered in towers and battlements, windows and ceilings. In the second half of the XVI Century, we had maritime interchange with the Philippine Islands. Twice a year vessels called *Nao de China* (The China galleon), loaded with rare objects, arrived at the famous Bay of Acapulco. Porcelain lions were transformed into larger stone sculptures and placed at the entrance of chancels as candelabra. Jars and chinaware graced rich homes, and ivory crucifixes looked down upon the silk gowns of the ladies.

The XVI Century comprised the printing press, the University, wise viceroys, communication with the Orient, eminent missionaries, and the definite enslavement of the Indian. In 1531, a few years after the disaster, the missionaries started the cult of the Guadalupe Virgin, with her Indian face and the December roses. It is a national cult and had political content in the hands of Father Hidalgo and on the *sombrero* of Emiliano Zapata, martyr of the agrarian cause, an unparalleled figure of the Mexican Revolution.

In the XVII Century, colonial art reflected Europe and adopted the baroque style of Italy. The spiral Solomonic column gave incessant tone to façades and altars. Cornices followed the decorative line of the columns, and above the dome for the first time appeared the cupola constructed in segments or in the round. As in the XVI Century, altars of the XVII and XVIII centuries are of cedar, goldleafed. Sculptures are of wood and their vestments seem to disarrange harmoniously in the breeze. The theatrical pomp of the church becomes exaggerated. The Christian church is built for multitudes, whereas the pre-Hispanic and the Greek temple were for priestly congregation and state heads. During the XVII Century, the churches multiplied and Spanish painting naturalized in New Spain. It was an ample moment of Spanish artistic genius, both in literature and painting. A young Mexican, hunchbacked, a University man, travels to Madrid in search of background. Juan Ruiz de Alarcón y Mendoza writes clever comedies in which the personages are not symbols but real people, with their unique singularities whether good or bad. His work sets a new date in the history of world theatre. In the second half of the XVII Century, Sor Juana Inés de la Cruz, genius of poetry, a woman prodigiously endowed toward a vast horizon of culture, lives and dies in Mexico City.

The XVIII Century was one of palaces and colleges. More churches were built, too. *Tezontle* (lava rock), volcanic spume used by the Aztecs, covered civil and religious walls, and in marvelous sculptures the stone spoke aloud in the incredible façades of the metropolitan *Sagrario*, the shrine next to the cathedral.

The Mexico City cathedral is the masterwork of colonial art, the most important standing religious edifice of the entire New World. It was begun in the XVI Century and finished at the beginning of the XIX. Its baroque style, of majestic elegance, made it unique, with finishing touches of towers in the form of colossal bells, and of beautiful cupola with graceful lantern windowing. Etched in the pale light of dusk, from the corner of Argentina and Guatemala streets, the two churches–cathedral and shrine – form one of the most pleasing architectural masses in the world.

During the XVIII Century, baroque came to full expression in a rhetoric of most surprising resources. It had one foot on the edge of the abyss. But it found its balance where this seemed impossible. It created, in scintillating perfection, a most splendid vision of humans and superhumans, existing within a style in which everything, absolutly everything, was possible. A country like Mexico with so long an ancient life, received the European styles with natural reservations visualizing their possible modifications. There actually is a Mexican baroque, unmistakable not only due to the material used but also to the talent with which the material was handled. And when the Indian artist had complete liberty, amazing constructions such as the churches of Tonantzintla in the state of Puebla and Tlacochahuaya in the state of Oaxaca resulted. For all that is Mexican is naturally baroque. It is seen in the pre-Hispanic, still extant at Teotihuacan, in the Quetzalcoatl temple. At Tajin, at Mitla, in what are called urns at Monte Alban; in the Maya (with the sole exception of the great cities of the Usumacinta); at Palenque, Yaxchilan, Piedras Negras; in Aztec sculpture, in Mixtec gold- and silverwork, etc.

The Mexican has great propensity for the ornamental and the magnificent. He uses and exceeds the flowering and the flower. Our indigenes speak little and say much. In the XVIII Century, in the Puebla Valley, reminiscent of the Orient a glazed ceramic was applied to the walls and cupolas with extraordinarily good results. Color and light. Color and light applied with festival eye. The tropic locale, without doubt, lent its influence. And in the highlands too. The Sun. The solar cult that once had been sanguinarily baroque. The *Guerra Florida*, or flowery war. *Señor, mi señor, gran señor* ('Lord, my lord, great lord') was the protocol salute to the *Tlacatecuhtli*-king — Moctecuhzoma.

Painting in the XVIII Century was characterized by mediocrity. An indigene painter from Oaxaca, Miguel Cabrera, filled altars and sacristies with canvases not always completely done by him. He had an entire staff of assistants and so preferred quantity to quality. He left notable works in Taxco, whose parish church like that of Tepotzotlan is numbered among the marvels of the great baroque of XVIII Century.

At the close of the XVIII Century and the beginning of the XIX Century, the icy ghost of Neo-classic style appeared in Mexico. After the large baroque sonorities came the false silence of the Neo-classic. A Mexican and a Spaniard shared it. The Mexican was talented. The Spaniard was spirited. The Mexican worked in the provinces, the Spaniard in the capital. Tresguerras, of Guanajuato state, left his greatest achievement in the city of Celaya-Carmen church. He projected it to its most minute detail. Undoubtedly he produced a masterwork, theatrically cold, white and gold (barely a dusting of gold). Neo-classic style — a return to the imperial Roman models — has no contact with Christian spirituality. Briefly, its expression was a reaction on the metaphoric cloud of the great baroque so passionately religious. Bursting verbalization was succeeded by opaque laconism. The most rare and costly materials were miserably imitated by painted plaster.

Manuel Tolsá, a Spaniard from Valencia, educated in architecture, came to Mexico very young at the end of the XVIII Century when our Fine Arts Academy was inaugurated. To him were entrusted the completion of the Mexico City cathedral (the cupola is his work), the planning and construction of the Palace of Mines, and the equestrian statue of Charles IV. The Neo-classic applied to civil architecture, in his hands, impresses because of the 'tonality' the great Spanish artist obtains. With a severe façade he contrasts the 'musicality' of the stairway leading to the beautiful patio's upper floor. A supreme elegance is paramount in Tolsá's work. At the cathedral in Puebla, as important as that of Mexico City, the high altar is the work of the Valencian master. To monumental feeling, richness of materials is added with notable color and lighting effects, the shadowy light much in accord with the purpose of the altar, to spotlight the reliquaries.

The Charles IV statue is another of Tolsá's masterpieces. Though this king was an undistinguished figure, the great sculptor presents him as a Roman emperor and thus invests him with a majesty he never possessed. The sculptor mounted him on horse, and the horse is the true majesty. Of heroic proportions, the work was cast in bronze by Tolsá himself, in one operation — something almost without precedent in the entire world. Tolsá, young on his arrival in Mexico, married a Mexican girl, worked exclusively in Mexico, ardently sympathized with the cause of Mexican Independence, and died in Mexico. A great Spaniard who belongs completely to us.

THE MODERN AND PRESENT ERA

IN THE SECOND HALF OF THE XIX CENTURY, WHEN JUÁREZ REAFFIRMED OUR political independence, the first great Mexican painter appeared on the scene. At the age of 22, he had already shown his capacity in the calling and his poetic gift in viewing Nature. Student under a notable Italian landscape artist brought to Mexico officially to head that branch at San Carlos Fine Arts Academy, José María Velasco (born in 1840, State of Mexico) had ideal qualities making him one of the greatest landscape painters of all times.

Nature as artistic inspiration appeared for the first time in China over two thousand years ago. In the XV and XVI centuries the Flemings and the Italians gave landscape true importance as a background for figure compositions. Then in the XVII and XVIII centuries appeared painters of landscape exclusively (Holland and Italy). In the XIX century, Turner in England, Monet and Cézanne in France, paint landscape with new hands, diverse techniques.

Velasco, man of genius, is a unique case in the Americas, referring to the field of art, in that the science of nature attracted him powerfully. So his published studies in botany and zoology show, as well as his observations in meteorology. But his scientific bent did not eclipse the artist, and from the roots of knowledge he flew on poet's wings. A few meters of eroded soil, a rock, the unstable form of clouds, atmospheric volume, light, then air itself (which perhaps before him had never been painted), impalpable material in suspension, 'that something' through which all is seen: Velasco put it on canvass or paper whether using 15 or 20 centimeters or three square meters. He undoubtedly allied to his attack on space an exceptional optical ability, a telescopic eye that devoured horizons. Therefore some of his paintings have cosmic value; they are fragments of the planet, not just landscapes. Before Velasco, landscape seemed to be seen as if through a window. The Mexican master chooses a peak in the Valley of Mexico and gives us a broad horizon in an immense focal cone. Landscape, but in the heroic grade, sublime. When Velasco paints the figure, it is always in relation to the landscape. But at times it has something indefinable that is deeply Mexican. Profoundly a Mexican, he immersed himself in our archaeological world and often painted and sketched it. He succeeded his teacher, Landesio, at Fine Arts Academy and thus became the teacher of Diego Rivera and other painters. In this way, José María Velasco is one of the grandfathers of Mexican painting. He died in 1912.

Hermenegildo Bustos was born in the state of Guanajuato in 1832 and died in 1907. He was of the indigene race, self-taught. He thought of himself as just an amateur. In all portrait work, the head is what is most important and, with the exception of the hands, the rest is accessory. Bustos painted heads. He really studied his models, and with rare intuition, he saw into their character and their way of life — the supreme, elemental function of portraiture. Thus the Mexican indigenes, *mestizos* and *criollos* had, through his eyes and hands, their real life expressed. All by himself he acquired everything necessary as a great portrait-painter. And he was this: an extraordinary painter. The first great portrait artist in Mexico.

The indigenist or Mexicanist had, at the close of the XVIII Century, a notable defender and commentator in the Mexican writer Jesuit, Father Pedro José Márquez (1741—1820). Among his works there is a study of Xochicalco and Tajin archaeological zones. This Mexican author was the first to propose the study of pre-Hispanic art, and at the level of Egyptian and Greek art. Therein lie the importance and transcendence of his work. In the last third of the XIX Century, the first indigene manifestations appear in Mexican painting. From Biblical themes, the painter went to autochtonous content of a historical nature and on occasion used it to condemn the horrors of Spanish invasion (Parra, Izaguirre, etc.). National feeling was beginning to consolidate. No other part of Indo-America had a XIX Century as dramatic as Mexico. Invaded and despoiled by the United States, invaded and oppressed by France; shaken by civil wars due to transcendental constitutional reforms, in a tempestuous sea from the times of Hidalgo and Morelos to those of Juárez, the country ran against the detaining wall of Porfirio Díaz' long dictatorship. Díaz, who first was an hero and afterwards the bad citizen.

Political agitation began with the XX Century. The miners' strike at Cananea, Sonora, in 1906; the textile workers' strike at Orizaba, Veracruz, in 1907; and mass Indian uprisings — all indicated to the nation that profound changes had to come about. The socio-economic Revolution was at the gate. Factory and field cried for human treatment. Liberty in general, and particularly liberty of expression, were demanded. The President, 80 years old, had spent 30 of these years in rigorous personal command. In the agricultural regions, what existed was practically slavery.

If Velasco was the land's biographer, José Guadalupe Posada was the people's chronicler. He was born in the state of Aguascalientes in 1852 and his spirited engravings were among the most admirable manifestations of Mexican art. If Velasco lived in air, Posada lived in the most human manner possible. He was sharing his life with his people. He was the treasurehouse of their actions and emotions. His engraving shop was a court where he, with engraver's tools and acid used on wood and metal plaques, imparted justice or supplied information. His trade tools withheld no secrets from him; they seemed a part of his being. Good humor was his handy small change in passionate tragedy and political life. This plastic chronicler, possessor of a marvelous language with which he judged, as no one else, society and government, is one of our greatest creators and one of our most respected citizens.

In 1909 Madero published his *La sucesión presidencial* (The Presidential Succession), and next year, the centenary of the beginning of Independence, on November 18 the revolutionary movement started. This was at the city of Puebla where Aquiles Serdán and a handful of other patriots were killed. In the history of collective justice, Mexico has an enviable place and fulfils her destiny. Mexico will fulfil it to the final end. Emiliano Zapata rose in arms to the cry *Tierra y Libertad* (Land and Liberty). Madero organized an army, the dictatorship fell, elections freely held for the first time chose Madero as president of the Republic, and thus the Revolution achieved its first great historical feat (1911). In 1913, Madero was betrayed to his death by Victoriano Huerta in a deal with the United States Ambassador. Venustiano Carranza revives the revolutionary movement, smashes Huerta, and reforms the Constitution in 1917 with highly transcendent ideas. Carranza was assassinated in May, 1920. The new government called José Vasconcelos back from exile and appointed him, at first, Rector of the University, and later reorganizer of the Ministry of Public Education. Vasconcelos, long-time revolutionary, outstanding writer and thinker — so contradictory in his last years —

marked out new and admirable paths in national culture. During his administration, the great mural painting started and unfolded, with its spiritual and esthetic message emanating from Mexico to the entire world – one of the most important art movements in the history of art.

A few years before the appearance of mural paintings, whose tradition in Mexico existed for more than two thousand years (Central highlands and Maya area, convents of the XVI Century), a young painter who died in 1918 at the age of 31, discovers Mexico and paints its people. This young artist was Saturnino Herrán, who swept into his work indigenes, *mestizos, criollos*. At his birthplace, Aguascalientes, in the old San Marcos gardens, he used to meet with two young friends, talking of art, searching for national expression that would provide Mexico with its own image true to its own inherent artistic richness. His friends were no other than Manuel M. Ponce and Ramón López Velarde. The former, our outstanding musician, the first to study our anonymous popular music for inspiration. The latter, dead at 33, one of our major poets, in poetry that had the tonic of the provinces' emotion. López Velarde, all Mexico in his profound voice, supported Madero. His poetry, Saturnino Herrán's painting and Ponce's music form the triple nucleus (with antecedents provided by Velasco, Bustos and Posada) for the creation of an art wherein that which is Mexican, our dearly-loved Mexican, would reach universal transcendence with national accent.

An extraordinary man, a painter and writer, observer and expert in volcanic science, revolutionary in everything, of highest human qualities, Gerardo Murillo (Doctor Atl) has chief importance in the story of Mexico's art and culture. For over half a century his activity had constant influence. Politically on the extreme left, Atl (meaning 'water' in the Nahuatl language) participates in the socio-revolutionary movement during its most exciting years. He founds the political newspaper *Acción Mundial* (World Action). He directs the School of Fine Arts. He discovers and encourages new talents. He paints, sketches, writes, produces monumental studies of colonial and popular art. He takes possession of the Valley of Mexico, plastically speaking, painting it in a spirit and manner completely different from Velasco. He painted murals in Europe and Mexico which unfortunately have been destroyed. Brimming with historic responsibilities, he was who convinced our marvellous landscape painter, Joaquín Clausell, to dedicate himself to painting. Clausell, a revolutionary too, was a noted lawyer who defended poor indigenes.

Francisco Goitia, great painter, isolated, but fructifying his loneliness with paintings of mirroring depth, and with generous cultural projects, is an unusual example of ascetic life. A Christian socialist, he gained his chief fame and consecration in the painting *Tata Jesucristo*. The sorrow of the Indian race so downtrodden for centuries never has had expression so tremendous as in this justly famed painting. Master of both figure and landscape, he paints little but his work is seen and noted in the ocean of painting flooding this epoch at the hands of his contemporaries.

The first great modern mural painting was done at Mexico City in 1922. Diego Rivera returned to the capital the year before, after a ten years' stay in Europe. He came back almost directly from Italy. Vasconcelos, Rector of the University, sent him funds to return to Mexico. I was present when Diego told the Rector that he wanted to paint a mural. Diego chose the rear interior of the Bolívar Amphitheatre in the National Preparatory College, and painted his gigantic composition on the religious theme of the Creation. He painted in encaustic and took very well-known persons of the time as his models. Undoubtedly Diego Rivera was born for plastic art. In childhood he had talent and by the time he was an adolescent, his work was astounding. He studied with Velasco for two years and always admired this master passionately. When 20 he went to Europe, on a scholarship granted by the government of the state of Veracruz. He worked and studied in Barcelona with Anglada and in Madrid with Chicharro. His painting hand was enormous. Orozco's was a claw. Velasco painted with a glance, Posada chatted through his engraving. Diego, who was born in Guanajuato in 1886, brought back to Mexico some of the most solid European influences: Byzantine mosaïcs, Giotto, Ucello, Ingres, Renoir and Cézanne, Cubism. When he returned, he found Mexico, first in the people's *retablos* (naïve votive paintings), then in the pre-Hispanic *códices* (the ancient Indian books, comprising splendid paintings and evocative hieroglyphics). And he found himself.

The artistic trajectory of this master is one of the greatest adventures known in the history of art. He was almost 40 when he rejoined Mexico. Here he undertook his maturity, here he developed it in one of the most glorious flowerings ever achieved. He finally created a style, his own, the Diego Rivera style. No known process of art was foreign to him. His discipline led him to master them all. But he worked most in mural painting and oils, and in these he reached the most complete perfection. Fundamental to his colossal output were thousands of masterly, matchless drawings. Luminous coloring dominates his painting, and in his great compositions a multitude of figures are easily discerned due to his clear plastic language. It is felt that his most extraordinary work is the great mural symphony painted in the dome and on the walls of the Chapingo National Agricultural College auditorium. Without doubt it is the work of a genius, a masterwork whose perfection astounds us. Almost all his painting seems to have been accomplished on some clear immortal morning. All is invested with the radiant joy of living.

But Diego Rivera was not only a painter of genius. He was a revolutionary, an eloquent and impassioned defender of collective justice. His verbal ability predisposed him to the narrative. Our history aroused him and he has left us, on the walls of the National Palace pictures of pre-Hispanic life relived with profound knowledge of the themes and prodigious color sense. The market scene, against the background of city and landscape, is one of those masterpieces unforgettable to all who have been fortunate enough to view it. A strange shadowy light circulates through the many-colored multitude. On the huge, monumental stairway of the Palace our whole history is narrated. Ingigantic synthesis, the artist gives us the pre-Hispanic, the Colonial, Independence and the Revolution. Life and drama of Mexico with a plastic force of most impressive grandeur.

Diego Rivera raised aloft enthusiasm and liking for Mexico's ancient art. He made a collection of more than fifty thousand archaeological objects. He planned and constructed the building which will serve as a Museum to exhibit them. Both the collection and the building he gave to the people of Mexico. He was friendly and generous, combative and brilliant. He had vast culture and great personal charm. He painted great mural compositions at various institutions in the United States. His capacity for work was unparalleled. He was born in Guanajuato City in 1886 and died at Mexico's capital on December 3, 1956.

If Diego Rivera as an affiliate of the Communist Party expressed his revolutionary ideology in his murals and writings, José Clemente Orozco — apart from parties though of the extreme left — again and again in sketches and political cartoons expressed his belief from early youth on.

Total independence in an area of tumult! Violent militant, incorruptible, definite and defined, implacable accuser of all injustice: such was the human and artistic image of this man of genius. The colors red and grey predominate in his work. Earth and fire: the base and the breath. Terrestrial man who internally is flame, impassioned man: Man of Fire. In Rivera's murals frequently the triumph of his social ideas is expressed and we are viewing consummations. His colors and light are indices of optimism, of blind and joyous faith. In Orozco, the sense of battle, the combative stand speak more of the present than of the future. Diego, generalizing, disperses in Humanity. Orozco concretizes man, what is terrible in the human condition, what is tremendous in human life. His supreme goal is heroism, the triumph over death through sacrifice. His is a manifestation of spiritual forces that no painter has expressed so strongly since Michelangelo. Gray is the struggle of all men amid hostile steel and half light.

On the stairway of the government palace in Guadalajara, Orozco has painted one of his most sublime works. It is a synthesis of the fight for liberty. The priest Hidalgo, father of our Independence, fills the dome, thrusting upward a blazing torch to calcinate the hated regime. A human junkpile emerges: a grey sea of men, human fragments, daggers and bayonets, industrial waste, symbols of betrayed and betrayer, professional highwaymen, 'bis lies' and all the possible horror of capitalism's sway. This mural composition challenges to struggle. You ache to join the throng in the street and carry the Revolution onward. The painting is an act of combat without considering the consequences but only the supreme goal. It is a rigorous cry of 'we shall triumph despite all'. A tempest at our command. Death as jubilee. The monstrous forerunner of liberty. This great mural, plastically, is superbly beautiful, masterly and original. Grey and black, white and red.

Prometheus, man of the earth who stole fire for his fellow-men, is another of Orozco's heroes and motif of another great mural composition, painted in the United States. Among his murals in Mexico, the one in the Supreme Court palace portrays fire and destruction as necessary operations. To renovate, you must first destroy. The torch to everything. Flames. Scenes of tumult. Sacred violence. Images of justice infringed, sold out, trampled. Judicial documents. A sea of wretched paper. All the color scale of the greys, and a tongue of fire flames.

When Orozco satirizes, starting the motor of his irony, nobody and nothing are left unscathed. All his horrifying humor cuts, grinds and chills both concepts and persons (first floor of the National Preparatory College).

Marvelous engraver, he left among many lithographs, one of calm silence that Mexico will always treasure in her heart. It is called Requiem, a funeral seen from the street. Through the open door, intimately, the poor people's sorrow. Only a sheet of paper, this, but as important as a great mural composition.

The image of death was one of his most continuous concepts — that which is decaying, that which will revive, Lazarus and Christ. The only landscape he painted was of the *Pedregal,* the volcanic residue, petrified fire, near Mexico City. He is one of the greatest painters of all times. Like Tintoretto, like Goya. In one of his last murals, at the Cabañas Orphanage cupola in Guadalajara, he painted the Man of Fire. It is a portentous work. At times you think the figure will penetrate the dome and disappear before your very eyes. This immense artist should have a ray of lightning as his signature. Master José Clemente Orozco was born at Zapotlan, Jalisco, in 1883 and died at the capital of Mexico in September, 1949.

An impulsive and monumental vitality, an exalted force for the noblest ideals of justice and heroism characterize the murals of David Alfaro Siqueiros, one of Mexico's three great muralists. On the extreme left, his ideology of collective justice, his competence in political struggle, provide him with necessary material to express in his murals his extraordinary power over plastic forms. His dynamism obliges him to renovate the mural movement's expression. His concern for a dynamic art and his search for solutions to achieve it have led this artist to the very frontiers of sculpture. His brushwork is as broad and expressive as Orozco's though not as great and bold as that of the genius who projected the Man of Fire. Siqueiros' bent to work in new materials carried him to the use of pyroxylin, whose texture offers new qualities. His favorite theme has been the dazzling personality of Cuauhtémoc. The young Aztec monarch is the ideal hero type. The story of Cuauhtémoc's life makes him a person so vital, symbolizing so forcefully the idea of struggle for liberty, that on knowing his drama and brief lifetime, you bow before his glory. No other Mexican artist has pictured Cuauhtémoc with such force as Siqueiros has. This most illustrious victim of the Conquest appears not only in Siqueiros' murals in Mexico but in Chile as well, at the school donated by the Mexican government to the city of Chillan after an earthquake there.

At the *Hospital de la Raza* (a public hospital in Mexico City), this master has painted one of his most important murals. Convex surfaces and right angles have here given him opportunity to solve problems of dynamic plastic. The complete composition is a masterpiece of mural painting. David Alfaro Siqueiros was born in Chihuahua, 1896. He is now working on a mural in Chapultepec Castle. He began his mural work in 1922 at the same time as Diego Rivera, José Clemente Orozco and Roberto Montenegro, the last named having his most important work at the stairway of the old St. Peter and Paul's College.

Mural painting has had other representatives among painters who have not specially dedicated themselves to it. Manuel Rodríguez Lozano, one of our best artists, and Rufino Tamayo, universally-famed painter, have both done murals. At Palacio de las Bellas Artes (Fine Arts Palace, Mexico City), Tamayo has done two large compositions on canvas which well represent him. José Chávez Morado and Fernando Leal are muralists, Chávez for his work in Guanajuato and Leal for his at the vestibule of Bolívar Amphitheater and in the chapel, Tepeyac hill. Juan O'Gorman, another of our best painters, is a muralist too, not only in fresco but also in large compositions carried out in rock mosaïc (the library of University City). It is one of the most important works of mural art. Jorge González Camarena is decorating now a wall at Fine Arts Palace. In the government palace at Morelia, Alfredo Zalce has recently executed notable murals. Fermín Revueltas, Pablo O'Higgins and Máximo Pacheco have produced excellent mural work. Pre-Hispanic murals of enormous value and lovely colonial murals are splendid antecedents of the great pictoric mural movement that began in 1922, placing Mexico in the vanguard of world mural painting. Rivera and Orozco left a gigantic legacy to which the other painters mentioned are contributing in diverse and important idioms, serving magnificently in holding aloft ideals of liberty and collective justice. These are the ideals of the Mexican Revolution, which on its march ministers to all Humanity's good. We hope that this great mural movement will not halt, and that new painters will continue the work that the masters so splendidly began.

MURAL PAINTING OF THE MEXICAN REVOLUTION

IT HAS AT TIMES BEEN SAID THAT MEXICO'S MURALISM IS 'A REVIVAL OF THE indigene' in painting. Strictly and justly speaking, this is not so. But Mexican muralism does contain a strong influence from the pre-Hispanic indigene aesthetic and in a certain way is its continuation, centuries later and in a completely different community.

Art in pre-Hispanic times was a form for the expression of collective ideals, yearnings and principles. Those civilizations had a strongly communal nature. Heightened individualism was not proliferate in them as in modern, liberal society. Predominant and decisive was the gregarious sense of existence, the social interest, in which all individual and group designs were articulate. This was as true in archaic civilizations as in those which had reached high levels of development at the time of the Conquest.

In the civilizations of ancient Mexico, state and religion were closely interwoven, integrating actually in a single force. All important expressions of the collective life adjusted to the needs and objectives of state and religion, which were essentially one and the same. Religion assumed a state, official character; the state, on its part, was an organ of religion. As a result, art in its most vigorous outpourings was aimed at the service of the state, religion and the dominant orientations of the collective life.

All evidence points to the concept that the West's 'art for art's sake' or 'pure art' was inconceivable in the ancient societies of Mexico. In the modern Western world, art is understood to be a luxury of the society, or of its directing classes; an entertainment of senses and spirit. But Mexico's ancient inhabitants did not hold art to be different or apart from their most profound interests. For them art was a vital necessity, a representation of the desire for life and part of life itself.

These ancient societies, in rude struggle for existence, had to exercise great economy of energies. In the course of thousand of years, they painfully ascended the slope of their social development. Their physical and technical resources were relatively precarious. While winning their place on the earth, they lived in perpetual battle with nature and fellow man. What at first sight appears as extravagance or lavish expenditure of energies — ostentation by the governing circles in the more flourishing civilizations, continuous wars and human sacrifices to the gods — had vital ceremonial function, whether political or religious.

This is even clearer when we remember the realist base of Mexico's ancient religions. They were not forms of evasion, of escape from life, but of ardent attention to life's requirements. Religion was at once communal ideology and science. Its symbols, mandates and prophecies were deeply united, from birth to death, to serve individual or collective living.

Deities were forces of nature and social life, as observed by the men and women of that world, or so imagined throughout the early and late evolutionary course, invisible and dimly evoked. They were not simple deities, nor were they idealizations, but represented the complex forces they symbolized, objectively real in their purposes — positive and negative, or both.

Therefore, since in pre-Hispanic society collective living was pre-eminent and fundamental, embracing needs and aspirations, art was not permitted to stray from social and religious objectives, nor from the will of the state. It had to be principally an art of collective inspiration and aims.

Another question — and the answer is more difficult due to the paucity of data that might completely illumine those epochs — is the clarification in each instance of the ideological content of their art works. We have only a pallid copy of indigene cultures, traditions, and compilations of knowledge and thought. Any interpretations as to significance of the monuments, sculptures and paintings must advance with caution and not stumble in the quaking land of metaphysics. The difficulty increases because in the ancient cultures of Mexico, plastic language was the supreme means of expression; all its elements (sketch, relief, proportions, placement of figures, colors) had exact meaning. Plethoric in symbols, that art was markedly ideological, representational of ideas on life and nature, whether in myth or in mysticism, transcendental and ceremonial.

In the definitely religious expressions — low reliefs of temples and pyramids, sculptures of deities with their attributes — that art exalts the vision of the universe and of human life which each indigene nucleus held. In other cases, such as the mural paintings of Bonampak, art expresses the power and dignity of dominant governing circles. But in all instances, art has a precise public function, it is vinculated to the state and to religion, and it invariably takes an active participation in their activities.

Thus the most ancient and vigorous tradition here is the organic unity between social living and art, with art as an instrument of expression for collective and state ideals. Fundamentally, the art of the ancient Mexican societies was religious, ideological, public, monumental, under state auspices and impulse. We have seen that it was predominantly plastic: architecture, sculpture and painting. Writing, an instrument of religion, science, history and literature, here had a strongly plastic character, the pictographic. Metal work, ceramics, and featherwork were equally splendid.

From all the foregoing, it is just to affirm that Mexico's pre-Hispanic societies spoke the great language of forms, volumes, lines, colors. We can speak, too, of 'the plastic sense' of the ancient Mexicans — it saturated their work and their struggles, their religion, their customs, their literature, their songs, their dances.

AMONG THE INDIGENE SOCIETIES THERE WERE DIFFERENT SOCIAL ORGANIZAtions but all had principal outlines in common, stemming from their millenial co-existence — in peace or in war — on the same territorial continent. Up to the time of the Conquest, the most vigorous nuclei had instituted considerably-advanced centers of state power. And these were not moribund cultures but, very much to the contrary, true progressing civilizations.

In these conditions, art reflected national groups, each with its own cultural personality and maturing process. From this point of view, each had its own art, corresponding to its socio-historic characteristics and serving the purposes of the community which facilitated it and used it for the community's objectives. It was a free art insofar as it did not depend for style or significance upon the society nurturing it. Therein, too, lays its unmistakable personality.

The Conquest violently interrupted the development of the national groups. In that tremendous shock, the aborigene peoples were devastated and all of them — confederates or antagonists — were transformed into a single mass of vanquished, oppressed human nuclei. The Spaniards shrewdly took advantage of rivalries among the Indians. To overwhelm the warriors and priests of Tenoxtitlan, who had established something like an empire, the Spaniards forged an alliance against Aztec domination. But they subjected all. Thus the Conquest levelled the varying indigene groups in servitude, and made them the basis of future nationality.

Immediately pursuant on the material conquest by intrigue and arms, was the spiritual conquest. Without it, consolidation of victory would have been impossible. The destruction of the indigenous temples, public monuments, priestly organization was carried out by the Spaniards with ruthless decision. It was not only rage. It was an absolute, immediate necessity for colonization. Everything that represented the ideology, the life concept, the socio-political organization of the indigene had to be obliterated. The very foundations of the antagonistic culture had to be destroyed. The old gods had to be overthrown and substituted by new. Thus the mortar that had united the indigenous societies was dissolved. Without a horizon, they had to accept new ways of life, a new ideology, new gods and a new social structure.

So we see the reasons of state, of high politics for the implacable destruction of indigene temples, monuments, manuscripts and relics, above all in Tenoxtitlan because it was the capital of the Mexicas' vast dominions. The destruction was calculated and furious. It was not idle, futile. It wrecked indigene society, state, science, religion, ideology and art. Of all these, only vestiges remained.

The indigenes, in their subjection, understood and explained their loss. They idealized their vanquished past, and moaned the catastrophe that the Conquest was to them.

In the indigene spirit, the impact was to be indelible. 'Feigning death, they saved themselves; all had been lost', the indigenous memoirs recount. The monk Bernardino de Sahagún, first and most illustrious researcher of Indian cultures stated: '. . . They were so beaten and destroyed, their things as well, that they no longer had any resemblance of what they had been before.'

The centuries-long gestation took place under the Colony.

Indigene art ceased as public, state, monumental art, and was converted into furtive, inhibited, domestic art of little reach.

Colonial art, succeeding upon indigenous art, was public, religious and monumental; but at least in its initial epoch, it was an art of the Conquest. It did not represent a formed, independent nation, but a colony in which the slow forging process of a future nationality had hardly started. It was not 'art for art's sake' — the Spaniards had no liking for this. It was an art decidedly exalting the projects and ideology of the conquering nation. It was an art destined to cement and lodge Spanish domination, economically, politically and spiritually, on the Indians.

The new governors hurriedly substituted the old indigene culture's forms and representations. They built churches where the *teocalli* temples had stood. They erected images of the Catholic sainthood in the hallowed places of the idols, which they destroyed or buried. In the principal city, as in the farthest regions, they built churches and convents profusely. The buildings were spacious, high, with airy courts and patios, of powerful architecture, functional for the new faith and for any possible military need. Sculpture and painting in many of them were very dignified and, in a limited number, of canticle exaltation. But while the ancient indigene monumental art (though only known now by its ruins) was a paragon of originality, force and character equal to any ancient culture's, Colonial art always seems a copy in the Western pattern, although with a certain unusual touch. And it is because Colonial art, in spite of attempts made to idealize it, is an expedient and partly a displaced art. It could not be otherwise, for the social entity from which it arose as still unformed.

Although the indigene peoples, vanquished, dominated, soon sought with remarkable vitality to adapt to the new forms — or better said, to combine their former concepts, institutions and modes of living with those the Spaniards tried to impose — they could not change their status of a defeated people. As a matter of fact, centuries were to pass before they would begin to integrate fully in the creative process of new nationality.

Thus Colonial art from the XVI Century on is admirable but precisely in the measure which reveals the determined effort by the conquerors and colonizers to deepen their domination and give it an aureole of missionary work. In her historic struggle to found New Spain here, Spain of those times dedicated considerable energy and talent. But the institutions she founded and the culture she transplanted inevitably were hybrid and second-hand.

A clear example is the disparity between the Laws of the Indies (a monumental archive of political and legal wisdom of the times) and the actual treatment meted out to the Indian people for whom those laws were promulgated. Many of the royal decrees as to the indigenes were of a tutelary and protective character destined to guide Spain's policy in her American colonies. But they were nullified almost totally by contrasting deeds. Now, in the light of history, it is vacuous to attempt an apology of the Vice-regal governments on the basis of the texts in the Laws of the Indies.

In art, too, nothing better than a collaboration between conquerors and conquered could emerge — and it was always a forced collaboration, the long period that extends from 1521 to 1821.

People speak of the indigene touch that gave a new and original air to Spanish-imported architecture, sculpture and painting. That is true. But the indigene touch in Colonial art affected only the secondary, form values of the works and not their fundamental line nor their ideological orientation. These latter were peculiar to the new governors of the early Vice-Royalties. Even the very Laws of the Indies, supposedly protecting the Indians, rigorously limited their artistic activities. Proof of this is the fact that still at the beginning of the XVIII Century, they were prohibited from painting likenesses of saints. Production of sacred art, in its cherished expressions, was long reserved — by tradition and decree — to the Europeans.

In addition, the Indian's adaptation to Western cultural institutions and forms was relative, not only in the Conquest's first phase but also far into the Viceregal era. Despite the violent destruction of their social organization and the virulent condemnation of their traditions and beliefs, the Indians maintaned their own thought, though hidden and dissimulated. This occurred with their religion, the high instance of their culture. In these circumstances, their contribution to the Colony's great art was — and this must be repeated — of technical character, and hardly scratched the surface of the fundamental orientation.

However, it would not be exact to assume that Colonial art in its whole transcourse was only that of Conquest and colonization. For the very reason that the Spaniards from the beginning had to project the Indians' pacification and religious-cultural conversion — in order to achieve their domination more thoroughly and quickly — at the same time they established the bases of a new nationality.

During the Colony's three centuries, struggles and conflicts never ceased. The conquerors, on setting up a block of private and reciprocal interests, had, while effecting this, accentuated antagonisms. Their *criollos* were the seed of opposition that with time would give to the insurrection some of its most illustrious and resolute leaders. The great mass of Indians and castes, depressed to the subsoil of Colonial society, continued certainly to exist, but only making its decisive appearance in 1810.

In these conditions, the Colony coursed a long era of national gestation, in all its aspects. A nebula of Mexico was taking form in the turbulent medley of concurrent social forces. Painfully her economic and political institutions began to outline. An unborn nation could not burst into a glow of culture. In lonely spiritual creation, the Indians, fallen and persecuted, employed their hands. The mestizos cultivated ridicule, ease, roguery and unsettling wit. Distinguished antagonisms battled on high. Quarrels between the civil and the ecclesiastic powers, disputes among the religious orders and waves of heterodoxy and heresy which shook the Vice-Royalties, marshalled the camps. The Colonial regime was undermined and awareness of the future dawned.

IN THE FIRST DECADES OF THE XIX CENTURY, THE SPANISH EMPIRE TOPPLED in both North and South America. Blind, narrow and rapacious in their own position. When new currents shook the world, they had to retreat before the onslaught of the Americas' revolutions and the hostility of rival empires.

Mexico declared her independence in 1821 but the destruction of the Colonial regime with its characteristic institutions was not immediate. The socio-economic structure, cemented and solidified for three hundred years, was still to take a long time before ceding place to the making of a new nation.

In multiple aspects, the new Republic's panorama was sombre and its perspectives uncertain. The criollos, the Indians and the castes (people of mixed blood) together had won independence for the country. But it were the *criollos* who from the start assumed power, excluding all the other groups.

The aborigene nuclei, descendants of the original inhabitants of the Mexican land, were considered as foreign elements, strangers on their own soil, for over a century.

In the battlefield of ideas, essentially and vigorously political, Joaquín Fernández de Lizardi had imperishable significance as the first Mexican writer to refer decisively to himself as 'a Mexican thinker', though humbly and lucidly. In his works and conduct, he sustained the thesis of the new nation's existence and its future under free and progressive institutions. The death of Fernández de Lizardi, persecuted and poor, after Independence was declared, reveals that his days still were not those of authentic national upwelling.

Struggles and upheavals were to invest the nation with identity, unity and temper. Iturbide's monarchical comedy was brief but gave rise to Santa Ana's grotesque and treacherous farce that engendered 1847's greatly tragic territorial loss. The Reform revolution followed, and the war against French intervention — two phases of the same consolidating process toward an independent Republic. In these tremendous episodes, Mexico lived solely to survive. The nation was thus long busied with arms and laws; little time could be given to arts and letters.

Of course literature fulfilled a mission in that half-century of formidable combat. But it was a social and political A-B-C of polemics between federalists and centralists, conservatives and liberals, patriots and invaders. Thousands of manifestos, pamphlets and books circulated among the people. It was a tumultuous literature of revolution and war, realistically serving the struggle and the Republic.

Those days of intense intellectual productivity left the Republic both the names of illustrious writers — Mora, Ocampo, Zarco, Ramírez, Altamirano . . . — and classic documents of dawning national thought. Yet the needful energy and calm for highest beauty did not and could not appear.

Art expression in those years was vague and unformed. The nation still forgot the ancient, great language of the indigene ancestors – monumental plastic art. Mexicans then only painted small pictures for churches or private homes. Popular imagery, naïve and delightful, took refuge in the *retablos* (votive paintings) and other miniatures.

The plastic art in vogue was, too, a poor and rigid academic imitation of the European. Very few Mexican painters of the time painted what they really saw. Instead, they imagined environmental reality with eyes fixed on Italy, Spain or France.

MEXICO TRULY BEGAN A NEW LIFE IN THE XX CENTURY. IN THE FIELDS OF ideas and of battle, the old and new problems of nationhood were debated: landholding and the use of land, rights of industrial workers, ownership of huge natural resources, education of the majority, cultural formation of the nation.

First, the Revolution challenged the old order and defeated it. Then, the differing revolutionary factions contended over the nature of the new order to be established. This was resolved in the crystallization of the 1917 Constitution, which conciliated the diverse revolutionary tendencies on a common platform, and indicated the basic trajectory of a democratic state. A few years later, when the tumult had clarified the elements of a new Mexico, work of peaceful construction began. The Revolution was to influence decisively the cultural transformation. But previously, culture had contributed also to the preparation for a change in the national life.

In the plastic arts, the Revolution's dramatic, noble and clear tone had been announced with exceptional eloquence by a people's artist — the engraver José Guadalupe Posada. He gained everlasting glory with his unique work.

Popular art ennobled, and won national dimension, in Posada's engravings. All his work is deeply Mexican: themes, personages, grief, brilliant scenes, even the bones of his living calaveras (the traditional skeleton figures of folk culture). His thousands of sketches were the first important treatment of his epoch's national episodes. Here the Mexicans are seen by the Mexicans, profoundly and in perspective, as they really were and as they wanted to be. In the engravings, the most frequent figure is Death, accustomed guest at the Mexican people's tragedies and fiestas. The Indian ancestors, in heroic love of life, had always paid him homage . . .

Death was invested with supreme dignity, in Posada's engravings, at the hour of a firing squad execution. This manner of dying — whether in the name of justice or injustice — was very Mexican, too. It was something incomparably virile, as if in a final manly act, the Mexicans wanted to redeem themselves for all the offenses and superficialities of life. Posada knew this in his very bones, and his firing squad victims invariably had a heroic stance. And all of them, whether innocent or delinquent, were men of the masses.

Great mural painting was gestating in Mexico's artistic activity from the beginning of the century. Yet it was the Mexican Revolution, that made Mexican muralism's birth and splendor possible.

The Mexican Revolution gave resolute impulse to cultural development, when it destroyed the old order and set the bases of the new democratic order. Culture had to rebuild, rejuvenate, reorient, in accordance with revolutionary principles and objectives. Faced by this artistic necessity, a nationalization of culture began, with greater intensity than ever before.

In the preceding period — the prolonged Porfirio Díaz dictatorship — the ruling classes had forgotten and denied Mexico. The estrangement of the economy corresponded to the estrangement of culture and artistic expression. For them the world's center was always Paris or London, and Mexico geographically was on some unimportant parallel. They imported culture from France and England along with their stylish clothes. All the while, the great mass of Mexicans were living with their own product; popular art, considered inferior by the upper set.

The Revolution brought the first program of national life to the people, whose material and spiritual interests resurged immediately. The people had never been uprooted, never sceptical about their own country, and were not now. In spite of violence and pessimistic prophecies suffered for centuries, the people believed in themselves, in the nation and in the future. They were the true root of nationality, the depositary of its highest values; they took part in the Revolution and so they revived Mexico from her ruin.

Under the dictatorship, the dominant aristocracy and the official intellectual sector had professed confused sentiments, a mixture of horror and shame, at the thought of ancient Mexico. They accepted as gospel the black legend that had been woven round the Aztecs attempting to justify and idealize the Conquest. They even overlooked those pages written by Cortés and other conquerors which revealed and pondered the advancement and splendor achieved through the social organization of the Indian nuclei.

Descendants of the aborigine groups had lived practically segregated from the nation's life, and were even more exploited, oppressed and molested than the rest of the people. For them the Conquest had not ended. The theory that 'the best Indian is a dead Indian' was maintained by some of the outstanding intellectuals of Porfirio Díaz' times, regarding them in crass pretense of alleged science.

But Indians and mestizos were the majority of the people who fought and won the Revolution. Consequently, even though not quite consummated, the rehabilitation of the Indians and of the values of their ancient cultures was visioned.

Among present-day contemporaries, Manuel Gamio evaluated ancient Mexico's art, gauging it at the same heights as any ancient or modern art. To this judgment, other representatives of advanced thought soon adhered, until finally this criterion was established: if the national culture was to be integrated, the valid and positive heritage of the pre-Cortesian culture had to be taken into account.

Then, too, the fundamental impulse of the Revolution had been given by the peasants, workers and middle class. Their needs and aspirations originated it, they bore arms to win it, and they brought to the 1917 Constitution some of its most elevated principles. In consequence, the new socio-political order had to base itself in these groupings, and the new Mexican culture had to exalt their work and struggles.

The present century's mural painting in Mexico appeared when a group of artists — revolutionary in their vision of art and social existence — began to paint the life and history of the people, under the auspices of the government. These painters had served their apprenticeship in the academies and the museums. Above all, they were direct observers of the Mexican people, fully comprehending its idiosyncrasy and sharing its aims. Too, they included in their concept of national art, elements from popular plastic arts which had been belittled or forgotten. They found a flooding river of limpid inspiration, almost an underground stream, in the popular arts: *retablos*, *pulque* bar decorations, engravings illustrative of *corrido* ballads, political caricature, Indian weaving's color and design, pottery, the children's toys. This broad current still demonstrated, though in simply-made, small objects, the enormous sense of form and color that had been a calling of the inhabitants of Mexico for thousands of years.

In these Mexican painters, art recovered its high category; returned to the cult of man and collective life; and assumed its full responsibility to the nation and to the world. The painter who held dialogue with his own heart and with the people — even as the ancient Mexicans desired — was again seen; he deceives not, he paints not in vain nor by chance; he does not disfigure the face of things.

To paint in the thoroughfares, instill painting in the national life, paint bibles, educate the people, interpret Mexico — these were the objectives propelling Mexican muralism from its inception.

Similar to great art of other epochs, Mexican mural painting has a message. It is the message of the Mexican Revolution, profound and visionary in content. The Revolution planned to destroy the plantation system, to hand over the land to agricultural workers, and to free them from peonage.

Much of Mexican mural painting is a hymn to the agrarian revolution, to the justice of its cause, to the rural masses who rose with the cry *Tierra y Libertad* (Land and Liberty), and to its brave leaders.

The Revolution also planned to nationalize the country's natural resources. Its Murals call for the construction of an independent Mexico, sovereign of its own riches, with modern industry.

The Revolution planned equally to strengthen national identity and deepen in the Mexicans' knowledge of their past and confidence in their future. The painters portrayed, on public walls, Mexico's history impregnated by proud national spirit. The murals did justice to Mexico's ancient inhabitants, to the liberators, to the founders of the modern nation, its defenders and its builders — from the most obscure to the most illustrious of them.

Landscape and light of Mexico are unmistakable in the painting. But what above everything distinguishes it is the presence of the Mexican people as central and persistent personage in all phases of their historic and modern existence: the Mexicans: of ancient Tenoxtitlan (the former capital of the Aztec empire, at the site of present-day Mexico City); under attack by the Conquest; on the *encomiendas* (land and peon grants of the Spanish crown); in the Colonial mines; upon the War of Independence; facing the United States invasion; in the Reform period and fighting the French; during the Porfirio Díaz dictatorship; in the Revolution of 1910. Summing up, the Mexicans in the past and in the present, working, suffering, delighting, studying, battling, and dying — almost at times disappearing as a collective entity or nationality, but always being reborn out of agony and disaster.

With ample reason, then, this mural painting is considered as the genuine expression of Mexican spirit, as national painting. Even when the strictly Mexicanist theme is forsaken, to treat universal content, the painting remains true to its national roots, since it views the universe and conceives it from the vantage point of our country's vital historic experience. On this road, detour from the truly Mexican painting passes the frontier of narrow nationalism and assumes a role indeed natural to it, that of universally significant art.

At the Chapingo chapel, Diego Rivera blended in a single plastic plan the Mexican people's politic-economic fight and a sublime conception of a society in which a free and hard-working mankind abundantly partakes of all Nature's gifts, through the development of science and technique.

In his *Mesa de la fraternidad* (Brotherhood meeting), painted in the United States, José Clemente Orozco limns prophetically the union of all races and all peoples in peaceful, just co-existence.

In several murals, David Alfaro Siqueiros presents scientists and technicians who have contributed to the unfolding of civilized life and to mankind's battle for health, well-being and culture.

The list could go on interminably.

This mural painting is the harvest of the Mexican Revolution, and as such has intention and a plethora of ideological significance. However, its ideologic force must not lead into an error. It is not, interpreting correctly, mere painted political propaganda. If at first glance, clear political and social life concepts surge . . . this is a virtue, not a defect, even from the strictly esthetic perspective. Mexican muralism in its best examples knows how to team elevated content with beauty of form. Essentially it is not governed by the wish to win proselytes for a given cause, but is imbued with the desire to ennoble the people's life, communicating through plastic emotion a sense of destiny.

Nor should Mexican muralism be reproached for making the man of the masses its hero and chief figure. On the contrary, this is a large part of its merit as art of revolutionary Mexico and the new era.

The consideration of the whole of contemporary Mexican painting takes precedent over any discussion of the individual qualities of its masters, however stimulating or interesting such discussion might be. All of them together integrate a pictoric movement stemming from the identical socio-cultural movement. In their artistic personality, they were each a product of the national renaissance projected by the Revolution. Their activities unfolded from the beginning along the lines of the Revolution's reforms. Among these masters there are distinct differences of concept, style, tendency, method and technique. In some, ideological message is more definite, clearer. In others, emotional temper has principal place. Still other give preference to sublimity and dynamism of forms. But all, and not only the most celebrated and most discussed of them, were related to a single current of mass, humanist energy. All of them, in greater or lesser degree, whether of real genius or only of talent, concurred in giving body and breath to the Mexican Revolution's plastic arts.

These works, reaching monumental proportions, were possible due to cooperation between the government emanated from the Revolution, and the peoples' artists. The state encouraged them, proportioning walls of public buildings to be painted. Mexican mural painting thus was a free art, image of a people fighting for freedom.

Due to this, there exists in the enormous quantity of Mexican murals, a broad variety of themes, styles and ideological tendencies.

The great creative cycle of Mexican mural painting has not ended, though some of its founders are dead. This monumental art nurtured by the people, by humanism, has not fed solely upon the genius of several outstanding personalities. It has been a movement of powerful roots in both ancient Mexico's culture heritage and the national revolutionary resurgence.

NOTES ON THE PLATES

1 Diego Rivera: *History and perspective of Mexico.* Main stairway of the National Palace, Mexico City.

2 José Clemente Orozco: Murals at the Cabañas Orphanage, Guadalajara, Jalisco.

NATIONAL PREPARATORY SCHOOL, MEXICO CITY

3—4 Diego Rivera
3 *Woman,* encaustic. Left side of Bolívar Amphitheatre.
4 *Man,* encaustic, Right side of Bolívar Amphitheatre.
5 Fermín Revueltas: Detail of the mural (encaustic). San Ildefonso door.
6—18 José Clemente Orozco
6 *Maternity* (detail).
7 *The aristocrats.* Main court yard, first floor.
8 *The trench.* Main court yard, ground floor.
9 *Ambushes.* Main court yard, first floor.
10 *Fertility.* Main court yard, second floor.
11 *The blessing* (detail). Main court yard, second floor.
12 *Trilogy.* Main court yard, ground floor.
13 *The laborers.* Main court yard, second floor.
14 *The laborers* (detail). Main court yard, second floor.
15 *Destruction of the old order.* Main court yard, ground floor.
16 *Thirst.* Main court yard, ground floor.
17 *The absorption of the Indian.* Main court yard, stairway.
18 *Cortés and the Malinche.* Main court yard, stairway.

SECRETARIAT OF PUBLIC EDUCATION, MEXICO CITY

19—24 Diego Rivera
19 *Poor man's dream* (detail). Second court yard, second floor.
20 *The burning of the judas.* Second court yard, ground floor.
21 *The Fair of the Day of the Dead.* Second court yard, ground floor.
22 *The exit of the mine.* First court yard, ground floor.
23 *The rural teacher.* First court yard, ground floor.
24 *The night of the rich.* Second court yard, second floor.

DOMINGO F. SARMIENTO SCHOOL, MEXICO CITY

25—26 Máximo Pacheco
25 *Peasant women.*
26 *Lunch time* (detail: *The grandfather*).

NATIONAL SCHOOL OF AGRICULTURE, CHAPINGO, MEXICO

27—31 Diego Rivera
27 *Revolution — Germination* (detail). Ex chapel.
28 *The blood of the martyrs* (detail: *Emiliano Zapata*). Ex chapel.
29 *Revolution — Fructification* (detail). Ex chapel.
30 *The agitator* (detail). Ex chapel.
31 *Fertile land* (detail). Ex chapel.

CORTÉS' PALACE, CUERNAVACA, MORELOS

32—34 Diego Rivera
33 *Construction of Cortes' Palace.*
32 *The Conquest* (detail).
34 *Slavery in the sugar mill.*

HEROES OF CHURUBUSCO SCHOOL, MEXICO CITY

35—37 Julio Castellanos
35 *Children's games: The little fish.*
36 *Children's games: The horse.*
37 *Children's games: The devil.*

EX NATIONAL CONSERVATORY OF MUSIC, MEXICO CITY

38 Rufino Tamayo: *Music.*

NATIONAL PALACE, MEXICO CITY

39—41 Diego Rivera
39 *History and perspective of Mexico* (fragment: *The three revolutions*). Main stairway.
40 *History and perspective of Mexico* (detail: *The repression*).
41 Detail of *History and perspective of Mexico.*

PALACE OF FINE ARTS, MEXICO CITY

42—43, 45—48 Diego Rivera
42 Central detail.
43 *Man masters the Universe by means of his technique* (detail: *War*).
45 Detail: *Victim of repression.*
48 *Man masters the Universe by means of his technique.*
44, 46, 49, 50 José Clemente Orozco
44 Detail of *Catharsis.*
49 *Catharsis.*
46, 47, 50 Details.

ABELARDO L. RODRIGUEZ MARKET, MEXICO CITY

51 Antonio Pujol: *Miners* (detail).

NATIONAL PRINTING PRESS, MEXICO CITY

52 Pablo O'Higgins: *The struggle of the Union* (detail).

UNIVERSITY OF GUADALAJARA, JALISCO

53 José Clemente Orozco: *Knowledge.* Dome of the University.

CITY HALL, GUADALAJARA, JALISCO

54—57 José Clemente Orozco
54 *Hidalgo* (detail). Stairway.
55 *Hidalgo* (detail: *Victims of colonization*).
56 *Sinister forces* (detail).
57 *Hidalgo* (detail: *The struggles for freedom*).

PALACE OF FINE ARTS, MEXICO CITY

58—59 Juan O'Gorman: *History of aviation* (details), tempera on masonite. (Murals painted for the old airport.)

STATE OP MICHOACAN SCHOOL, MEXICO CITY

60—63 Pablo O'Higgins
60 *Public demonstration.*
61 *Dispossession of laborers.*
62 *Ball players.*
63 *School.*

CABAÑAS ORPHANAGE, GUADALAJARA, JALISCO

64—70 José Clemente Orozco
64 *Conquest.*
65 *Confussion of religions* (detail).
66 *Two-headed horses.*
67 *The poor artist.*
68 *Dream, contemplation, dominion: The flame of the spirit.*
69 *The iron man.*
70 *Threats.*

GABINO ORTIZ LIBRARY, Jiquilpan, MICHOACAN

71—73 José Clemente Orozco
71 *Allegory of Mexico* (detail).
72 *Allegory of Mexico.*
73 Frontal wall of the presbytery.

SUPREME COURT OF JUSTICE, MEXICO CITY

74—77 José Clemente Orozco
74 *Justice* (detail).
75 *Inhuman work.*
76—77 *Justice* (details).

JESUS HOSPITAL, MEXICO CITY

78—81 José Clemente Orozco
78 *Vision of the Apocalypse* (detail: *Pity*). Chapel's choir loft.
79 *Vision of the Apocalypse* (detail: *Apocalyptical prostitute*). Chapel's arch.
80 *Vision of the Apocalypse* (detail: *Liberation of Satan*). Chapel's arch.
81 *Vision of the Apocalypse* (detail: *The demon in bonds*). Chapel's choir loft.

GERTRUDIS BOCANEGRA LIBRARY, PATZCUARO, MICHOACAN

82—84 Juan O'Gorman
82 Mural.
83—84 Details of mural.

NATIONAL INSTITUTE OF CARDIOLOGY, MEXICO CITY

85—86 Diego Rivera
85 *History of cardiology.*
86 *Servet, Martyr of science* (detail).

NATIONAL PALACE (SECOND FLOOR CORRIDORS), MEXICO CITY

87—96 Diego Rivera
87 *Great Tenochtitlán. The Market.*
88 Detail from *The Market.*
89 Detail from *The Weavers of Sleeping mats.*
90 *Colonial domination* (detail).
91 *Colonial domination.*
92 *Colonial domination* (detail).
93 *Totonacan civilization* (detail).
94 *Totonacan civilization* (detail: *The glying pole*).
95 *Corn* (detail).
96 *Pulque.*

JOSE CLEMENTE OROZCO MUSEUM, GUADALAJARA, JALISCO

97—99 José Clemente Orozco: (Murals painted for the Turf Club of Mexico City).
97 *La joie de vivre*, vinelite (detail).
98 *La joie de vivre*, vinelite.
99 *La joie de vivre*, vinelite (detail).

PALACE OF FINE ARTS, MEXICO CITY

100—102 David Alfaro Siqueiros
100 *New democracy*, pyroxiline. Detail of central wall.
101 *New democracy*, pyroxiline. Central wall.
102 *New democracy*, pyroxiline. Detail of right mural. Central wall.

NATIONAL MUSEUM OF HISTORY, CHAPULTEPEC, MEXICO CITY

103—105 José Clemente Orozco
103 *Juárez and The defeat of the Empire* (detail: *The political clergy*).
104 *Juárez and the defeat of the Empire* (detail: *The emperor's corpse*).
105 *Juárez and the defeat of the Empire.*
106—107 Leopoldo Méndez and Pablo O'Higgins: *Social aid* (details).

CITY HALL, GUADALAJARA, JALISCO

108—110 José Clemente Orozco
108—109 *Abolition of slavery* (details). Arch of the House of Representatives.
110 Detail: *Hidalgo.*

DEL PRADO HOTEL, MEXICO CITY

111—116 Diego Rivera
111 *Sunday afternoon dream at the Central Alameda* (detail: *regressive self-portrait*).
112 Detail.
113 Detail: *Social classes in the days of President Porfirio Díaz.*
114 Detail: *A dandy skull.*
115 Detail: *The rich girl.*
116 Detail: *The poor girl.*

CHAMBER OF DISTRIBUTION OF THE LERMA WATER SUPPLY, MEXICO CITY

117—119 Diego Rivera: *Water and life* (details), polyestirene.

REGIONAL MUSEUM OF ANTHROPOLOGY AND HISTORY, MORELIA, MICHOACAN

120, 122 Alfredo Zalce
120 *Cuauhtémoc, symbol of nationality.*
122 *People of the world against atomic war.*

CITY HALL, MORELIA, MICHOACAN

121 Alfredo Zalce: *The liberators:* Stairway.

LIFE AND WORK OF IGNACIO ALLENDE, SAN MIGUEL ALLENDE, GUANAJUATO

123 David Alfaro Siqueiros: *Life and work of Ignacio Allende*, example of polyangular stroke. Synthetic materials.

PALACE OF FINE ARTS, MEXICO CITY

124—125 Rufino Tamayo
124 *Mexico today* (detail). Vinelite on canvas.
125 *Birth of our nationality* (detail). Vinelite on canvas.
126 David Alfaro Siqueiros: *Cuauhtémoc Resurrected*
126 David Alfaro Siqueiros: *Cuauhtémoc Resurrected* (detail). Synthetic materials.

PUBLIC GRANARY (ALHONDIGA DE GRANADITAS) GUANAJUATO, GUANAJUATO

127—129 José Chávez Morado
127 *Cuauhtémoc and the Conquest* (detail).
128 *End of viceroyship.*
129 *The liberator of Hidalgo.*

HOUSE OF SENATORS, MEXICO CITY

130—131 Jorge González Camarena
130 *Revolution and Constitution of 1917* (fragment), synthetic materials.
131 *Independence and Reform* (fragment), synthetic materials.

HOSPITAL OF THE RACE, MEXICO CITY

132—134 David Alfaro Siqueiros
132 *For an absolute security for Mexicans* (detail), pyroxiline.
133 Detail: *Labor accident.*
134 Detail: *The Harvest.*
135 *Ancient and modern medicine* (detail: *Miners*).
136—140 *Ancient and modern medicine* (details).

MEDICAL CENTER, MEXICO CITY

141—143 David Alfaro Siqueiros: *Apology of the future triumph of science over cancer* (details), pyroxiline.

NATIONAL MUSEUM OF HISTORY, CHAPULTEPEC, MEXICO CITY

144—147 David Alfaro Siqueiros
144 *The Revolution against the dictatorship of Porfirio Díaz* (details: *Porfirio Díaz, the dictator*), pyroxiline.
145—147 *The Revolution against the dictatorship of Porfirio Díaz* (details: *The strike at Cananea*), pyroxiline.

First cover: Diego Rivera: *Revolution — Germination* (detail), (see explanation of plate no. 27).

Fourth cover: José Clemente Orozco: *Inhuman labor*, mural at the Supreme Court of Justice, Mexico City.

Flyleaf: Tlaloc, God of Rain, fresco — Teotihuacan culture — III—IX centuries A.D.

The Editors wish to express their sincerest gratitude for the assistance given to them by numerous persons in allowing them to reproduce the drawings, sketches, plans and photographs of their private collections. They also acknowledge their gratefulness to the President of the Supreme Court of the Nation, the Secretaries of State, the Directors of the Institutes, the Deans of the Universities and the Governors of different States for their cooperation in the reproduction of murals of the buildings under their respective jurisdictions.

The printing of this book was finished in March, 1967 at the Artia Printing Shop (Czechoslovakia). This edition consists of 2,500 copies.

TIERRA Y

HUELGA

3

4

7

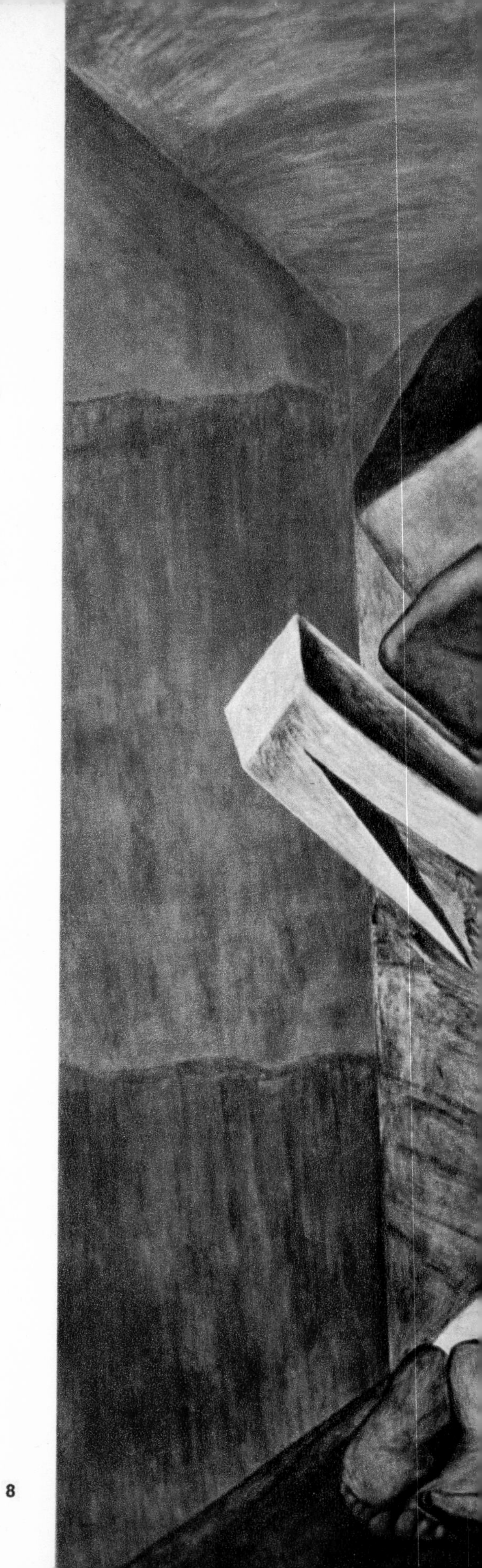

10

11

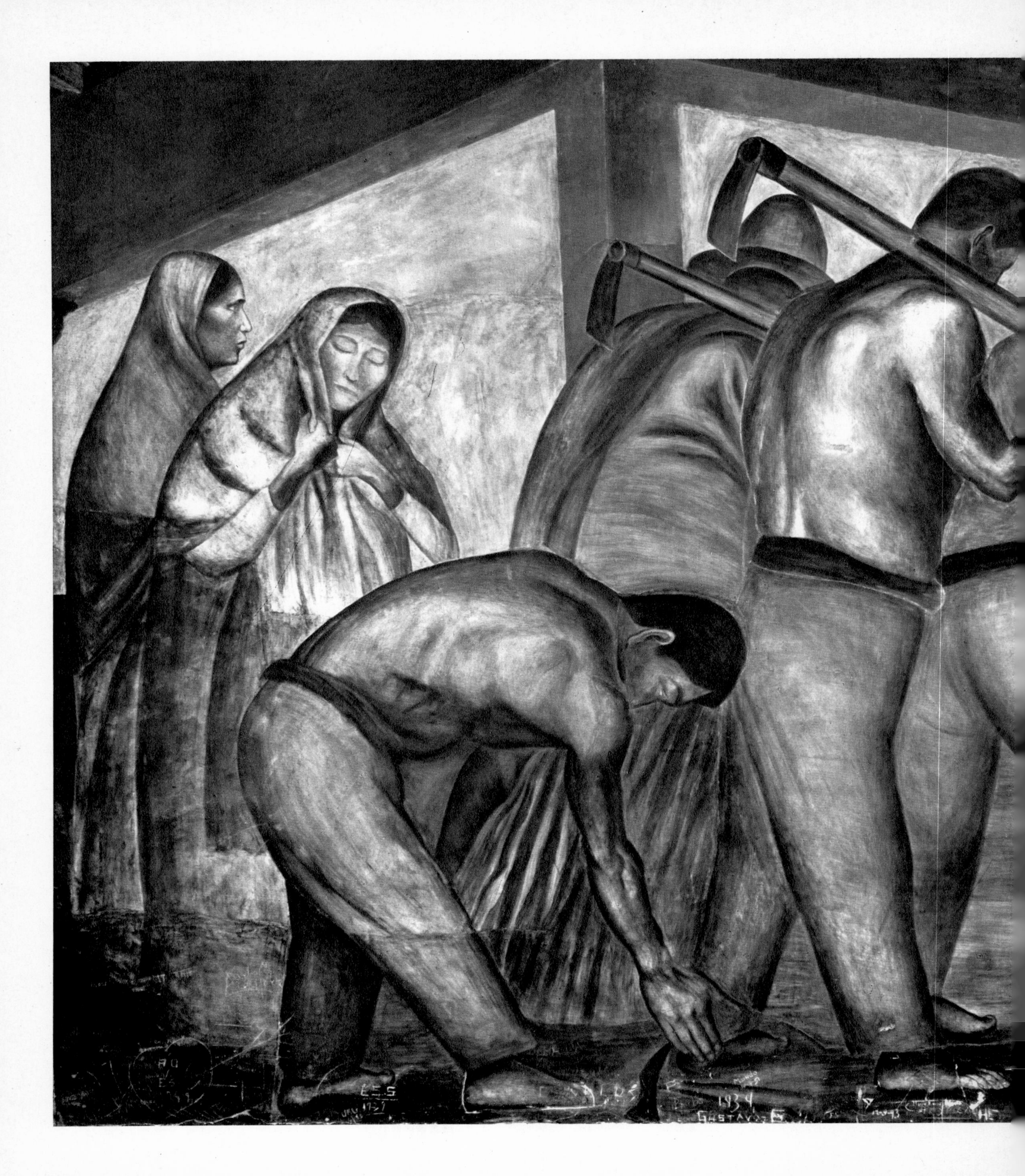

14

15

17

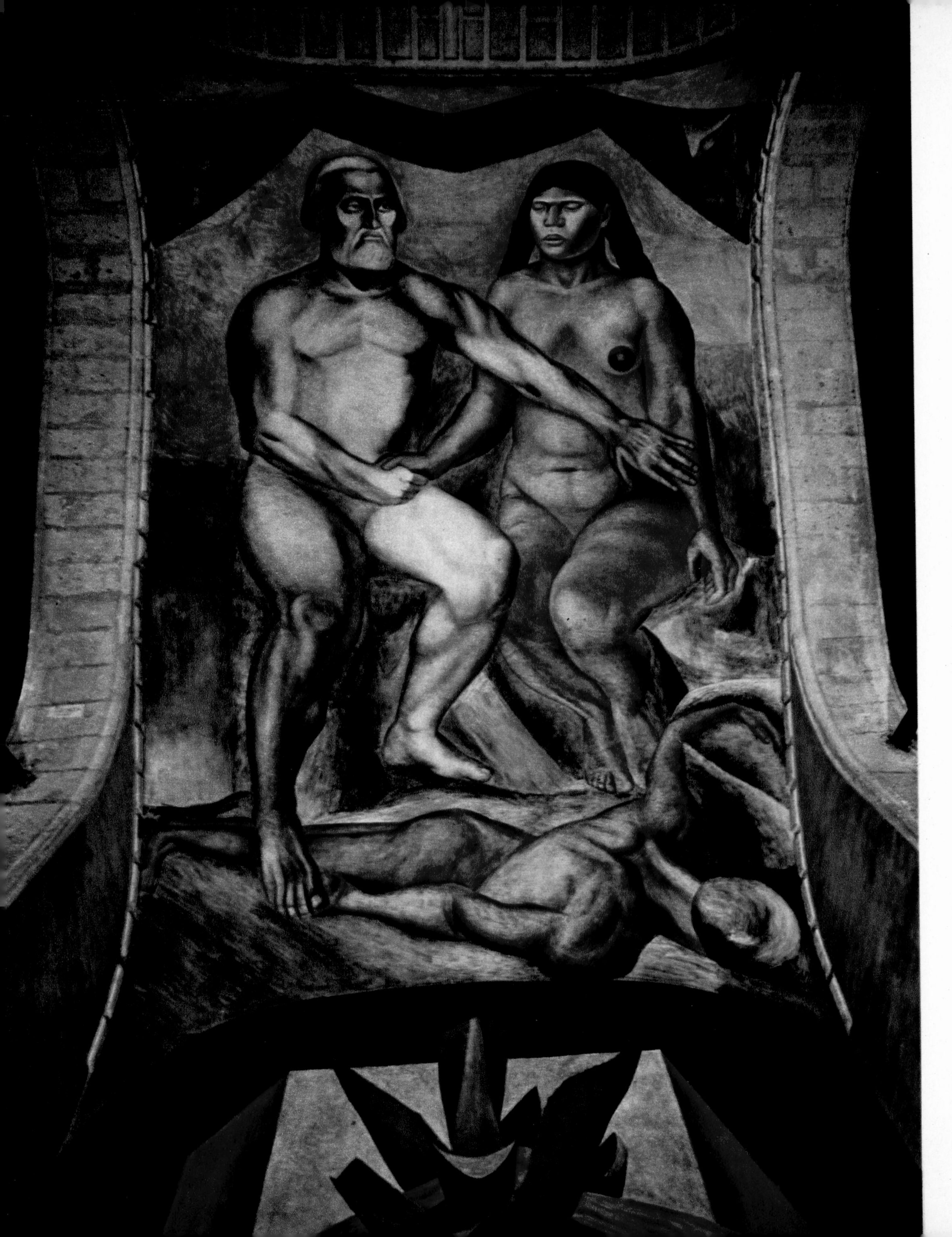

18

22

23

que todos los
pesos
duros
Es

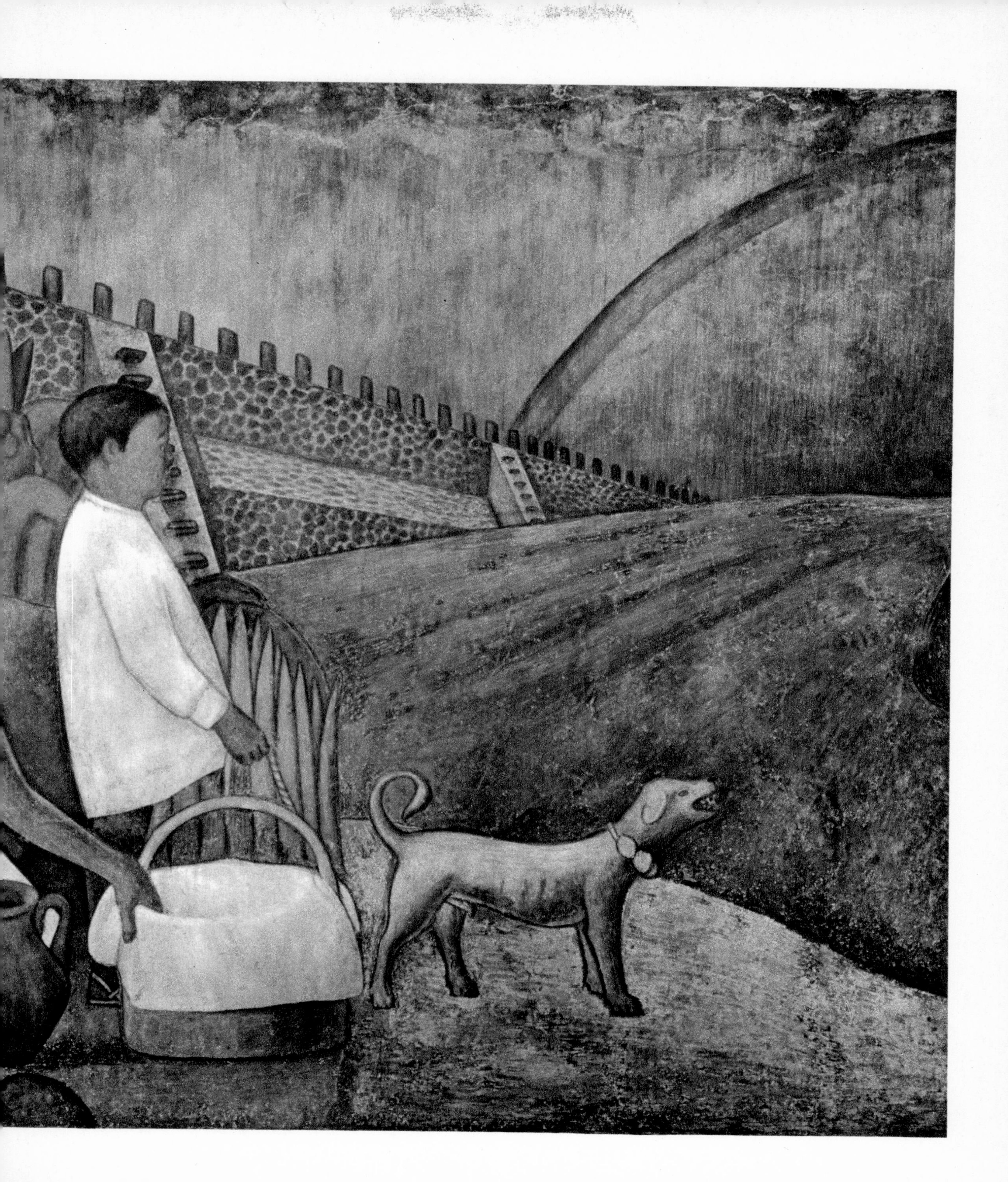

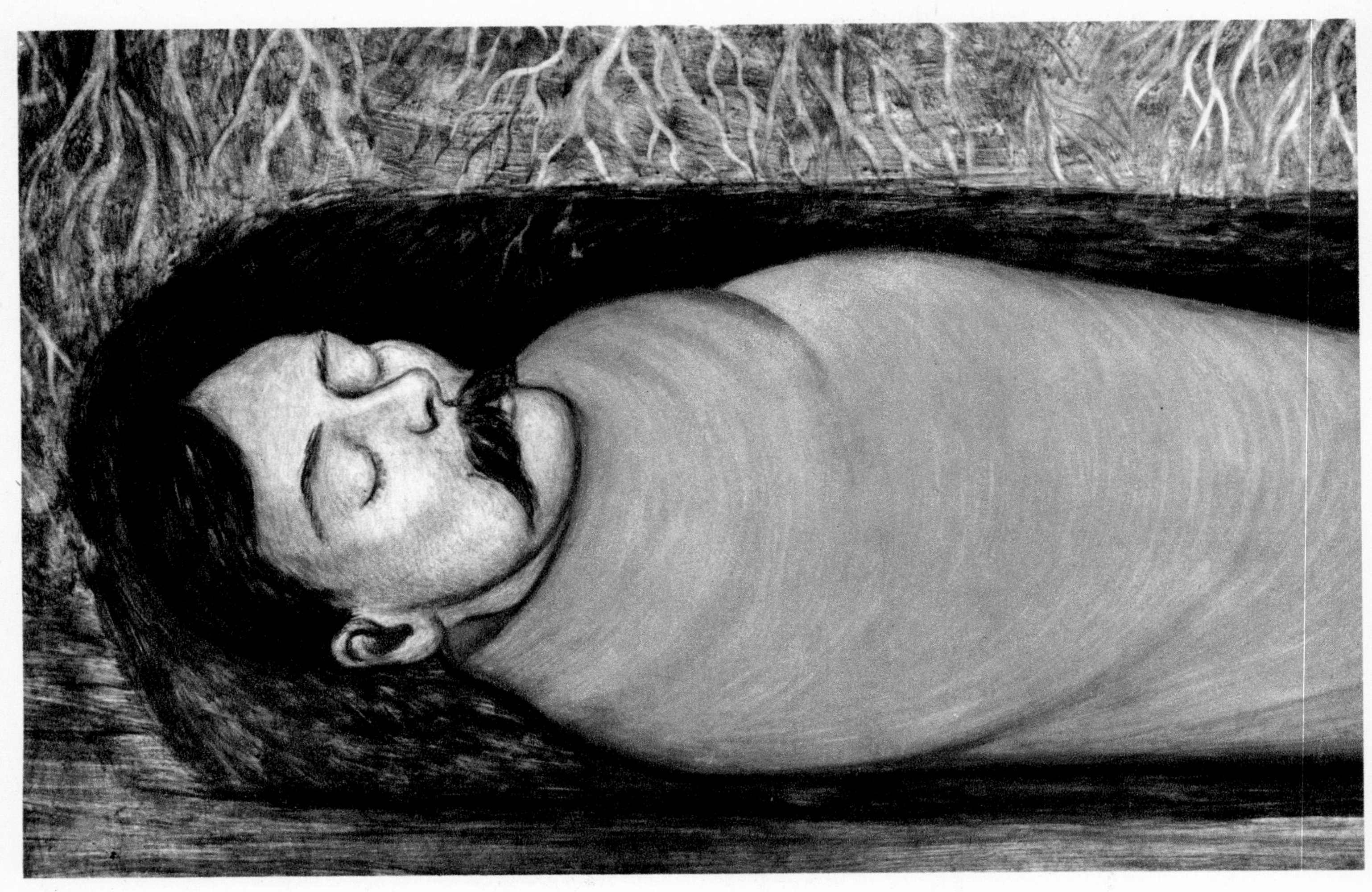

28

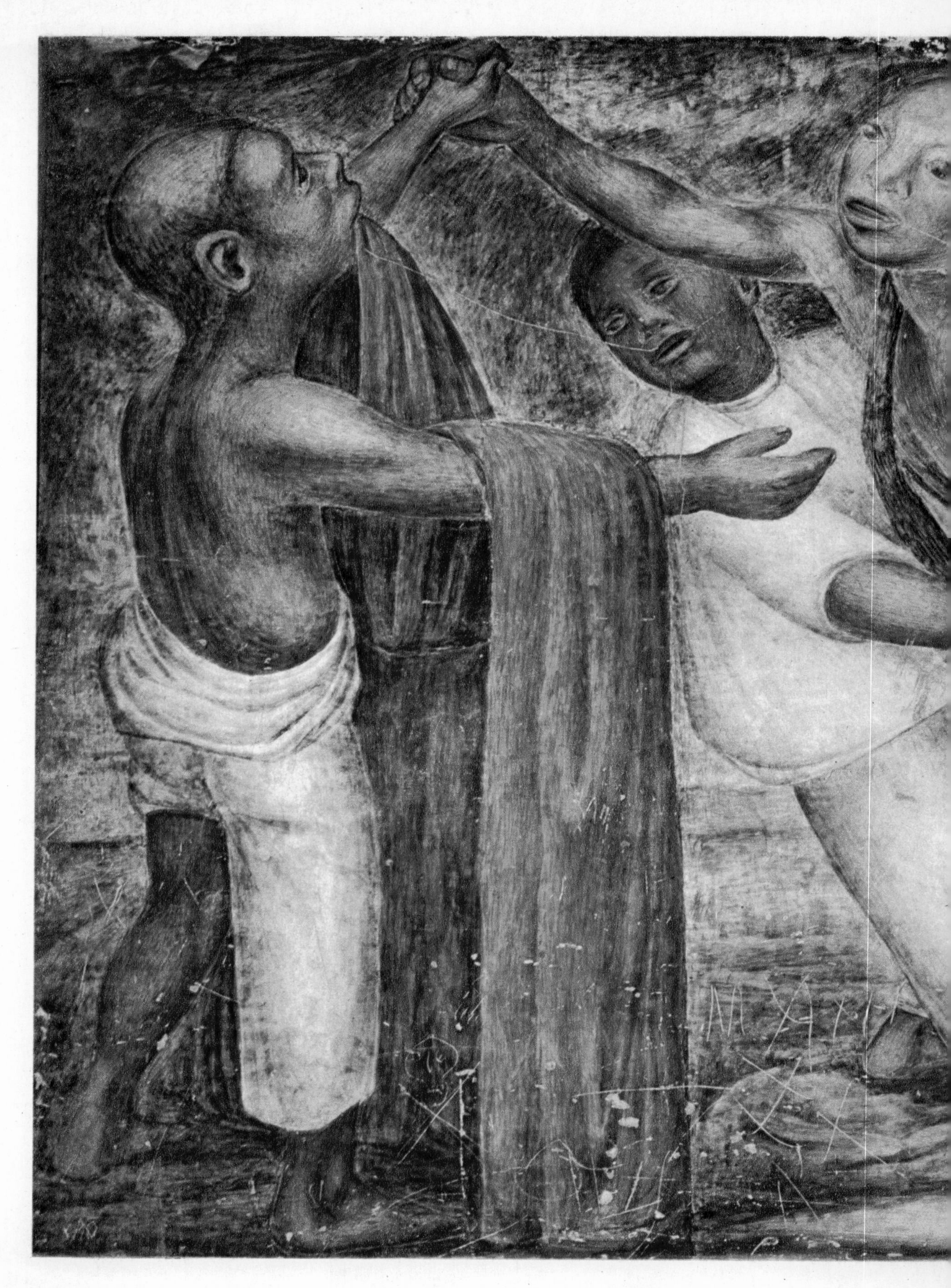

37

TIERRA Y LI
ERTAD

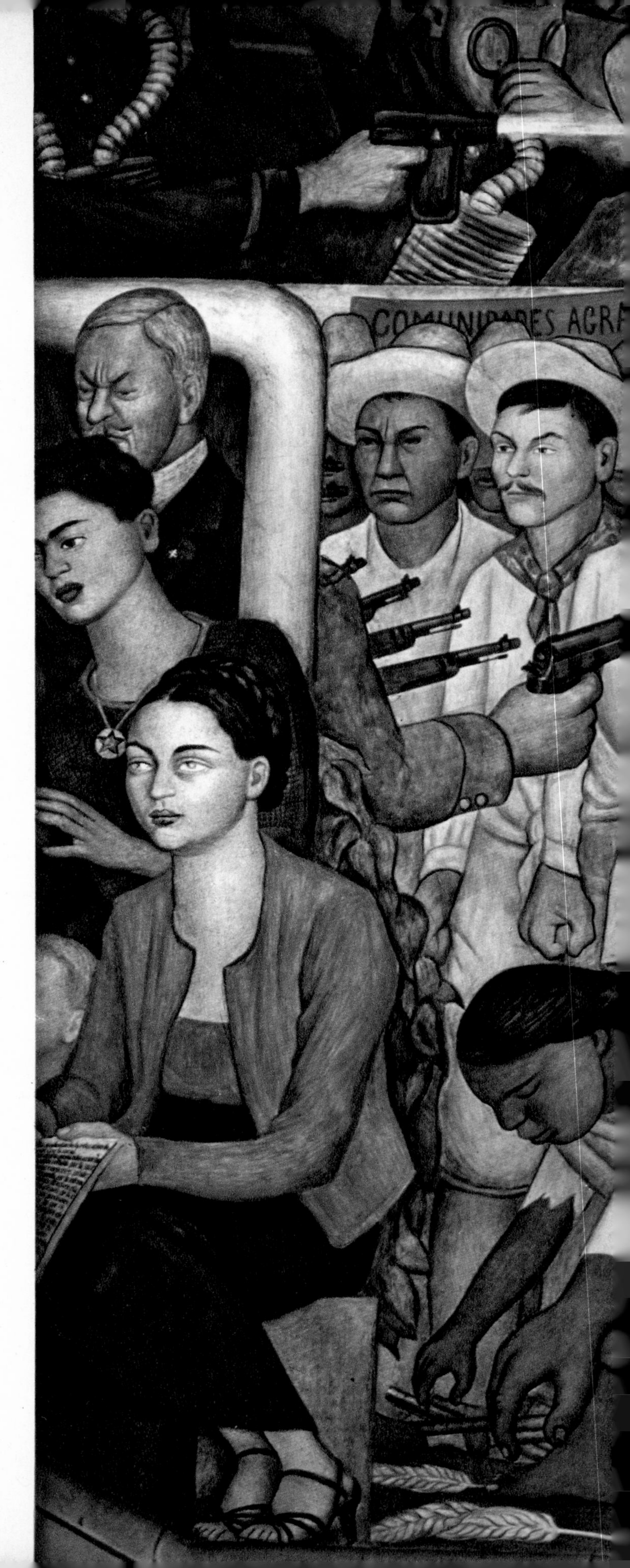
COMUNIDADES AGRA

CABALLEROS
DE COLON

50

For technical reasons
the illustrations nos 48 and 49
have been placed
following the illustration no 56.

57

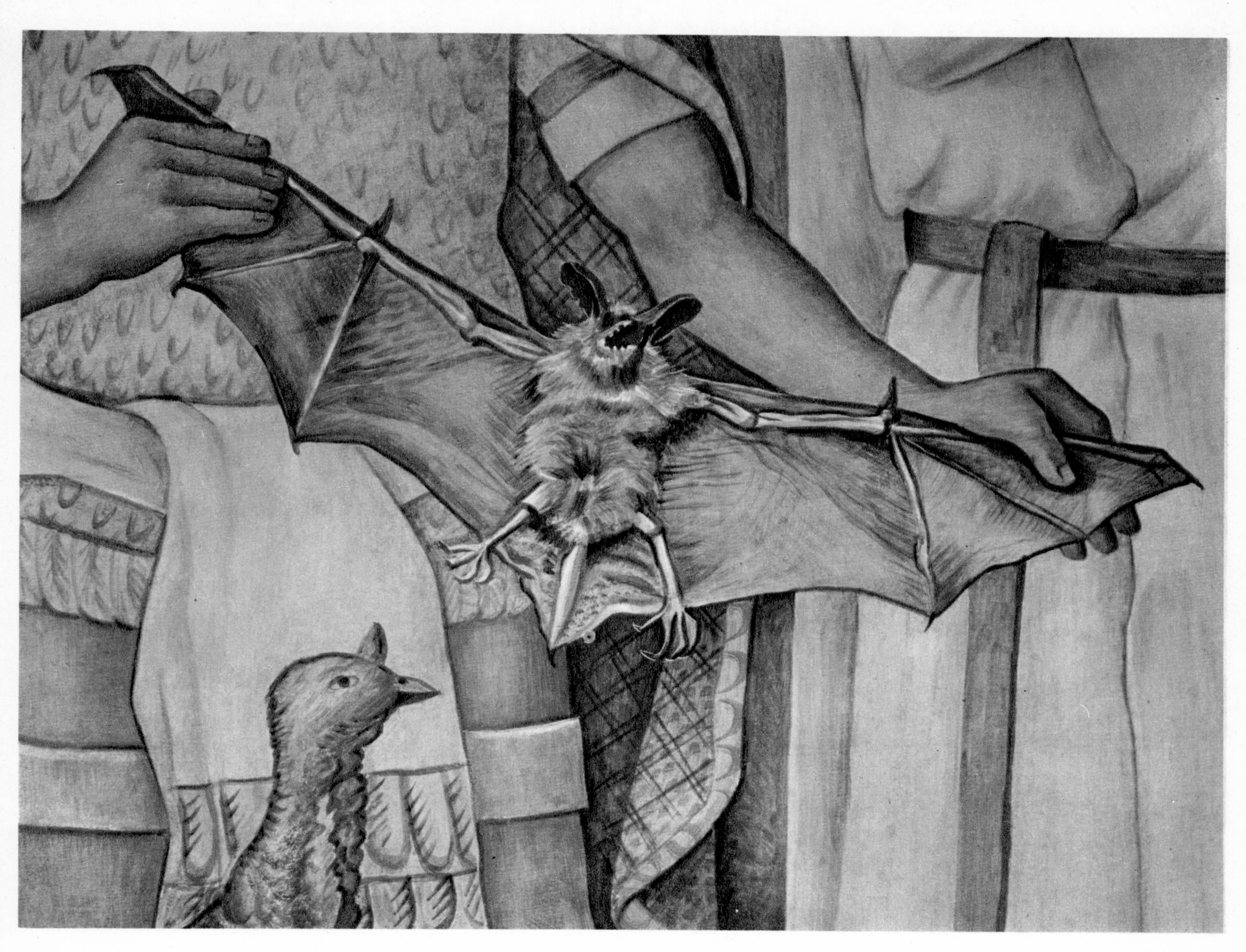

59

61

71

74

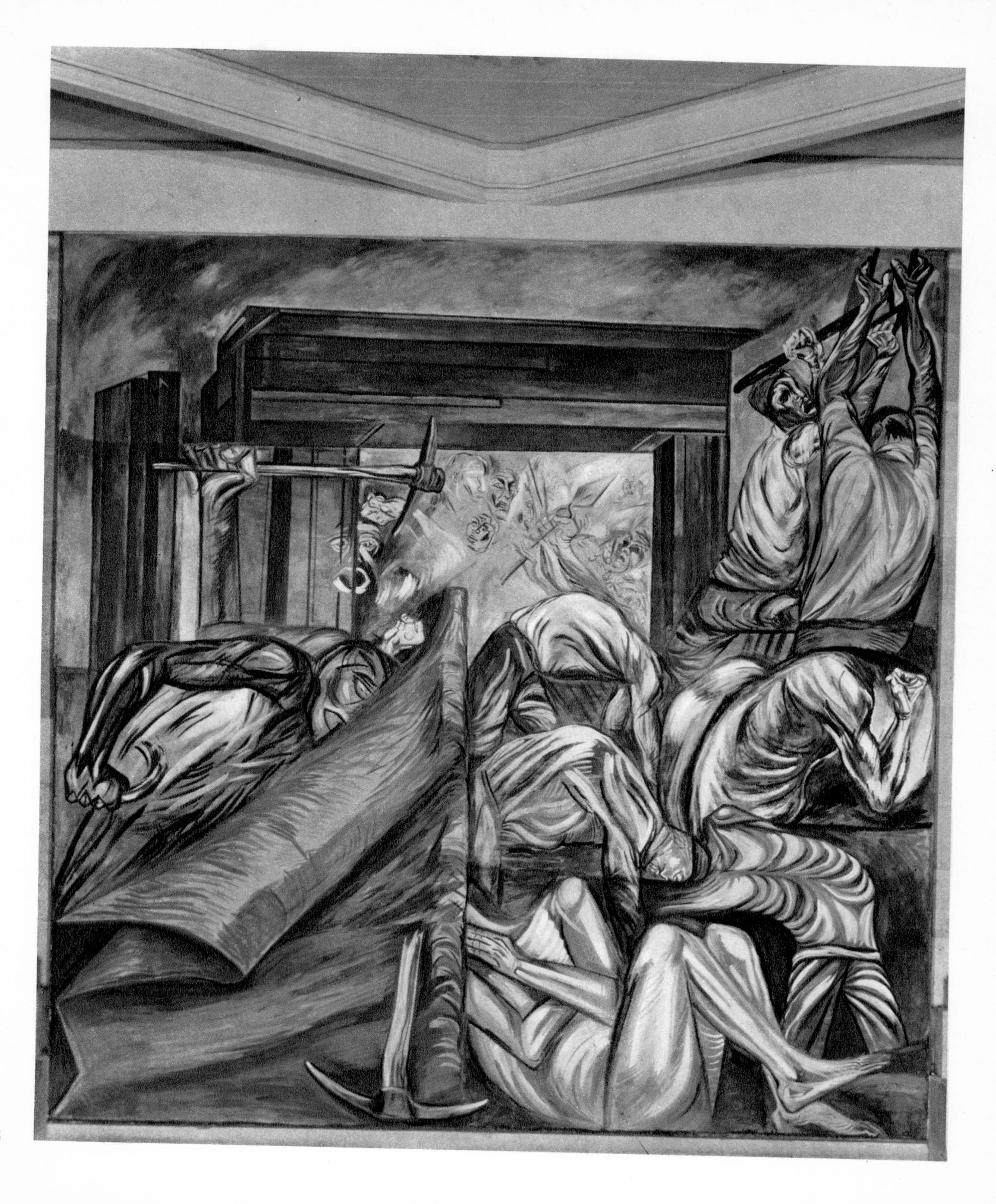

75

80

UTOPIA

Han pasado
No han muerto de hambre
Han labrado la tierra con sus
manos para darnos de comer
Les robaron sus tesoros
como un gigantesco
volcán en erupción.
Tangaxoan II ultim
monarca de los Indi
Purepecha fue tortur
y asesinado por las fer
hordas conducidas por
sádico: vil Nuño de Guzm
Los conquistadores
martirizaron, robaron,
humillaron a los indios
y los convirtieron en
siervos, esclavos o en
mendigos y pordioseros

TIERRA
Y LIBERTAD
INDEPENDENCIA
Y LIBERTAD
PARA TODOS
LOS PUEBLOS
DE LAS
AMERICAS
Me Gertrudis
Bocanegra
dio su sangre por
La Independencia

RENE THÉOPHILE-HYACINTHE
LAËNNEC
(1781-1826)
MORGAGNI
WILLIAM
HARVEY
(1578-1657)
SAINTE
BIBLE
CLAUDIO·GALENO
ANDRES
VESALIUS

MEDICINA CHINA
ANTERIOR A LA ERA CRIS-
TIANA

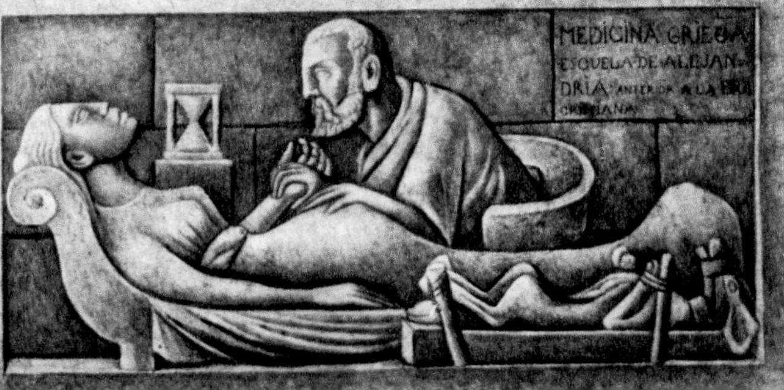
MEDICINA GRIEGA

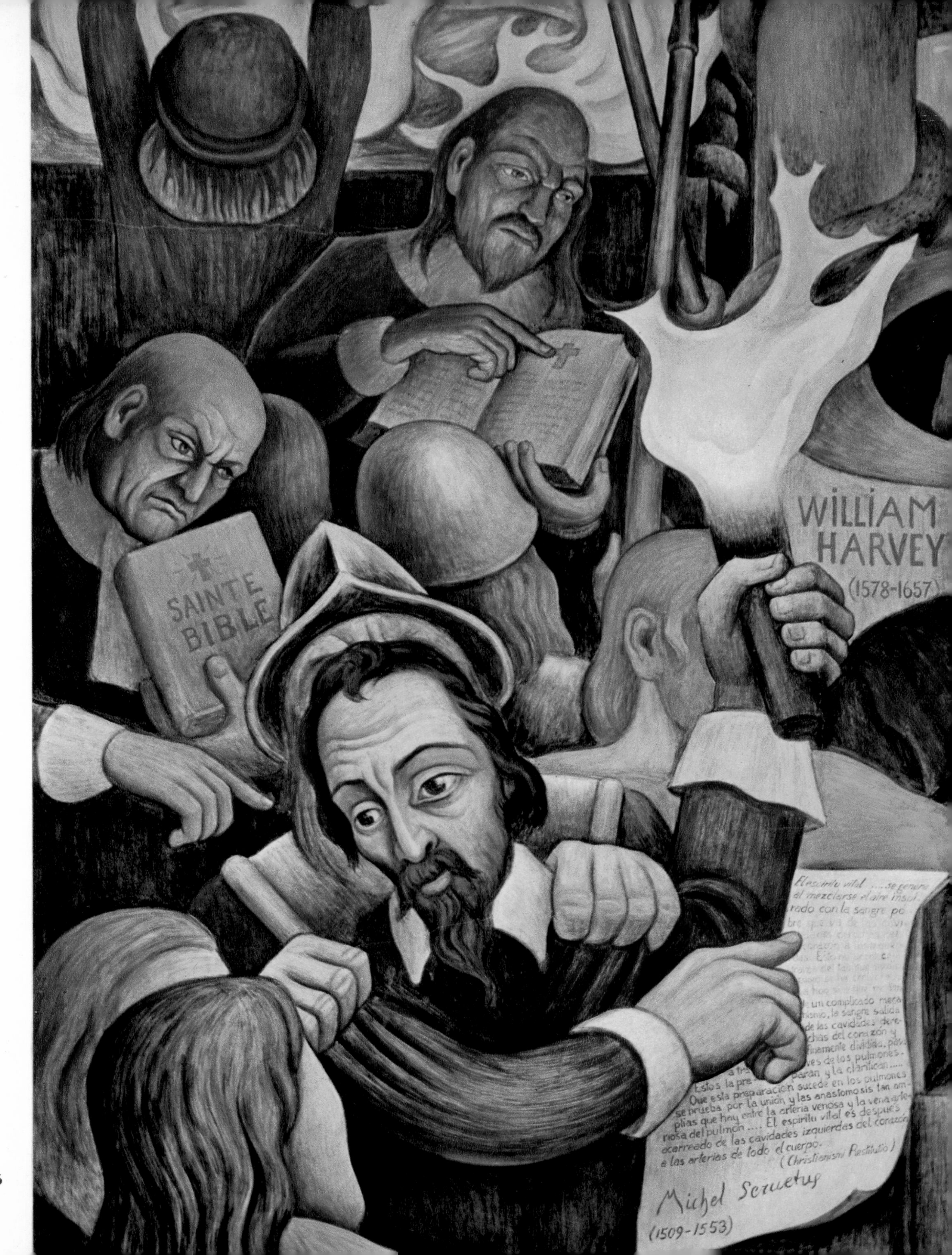

WILLIAM
HARVEY
(1578-1657)
SAINTE
BIBLE
El espiritu vital ....se genera
al mezclarse el aire inspi-
rado con la sangre po
un complicado meca-
nismo, la sangre salida
de las cavidades dere-
chas del corazón y
ves de los pulmones.
paran y la clarifican....
Estos la pre
Que esta preparación sucede en los pulmones
se prueba por la unión y las anastomosis tan am-
plias que hay entre la arteria venosa y la vena arte-
riosa del pulmón .... El espiritu vital es después
acarreado de las cavidades izquierdas del corazón
a las arterias de todo el cuerpo.
(Christianismi Restitutio)
Michel Servetus
(1509-1553)

88

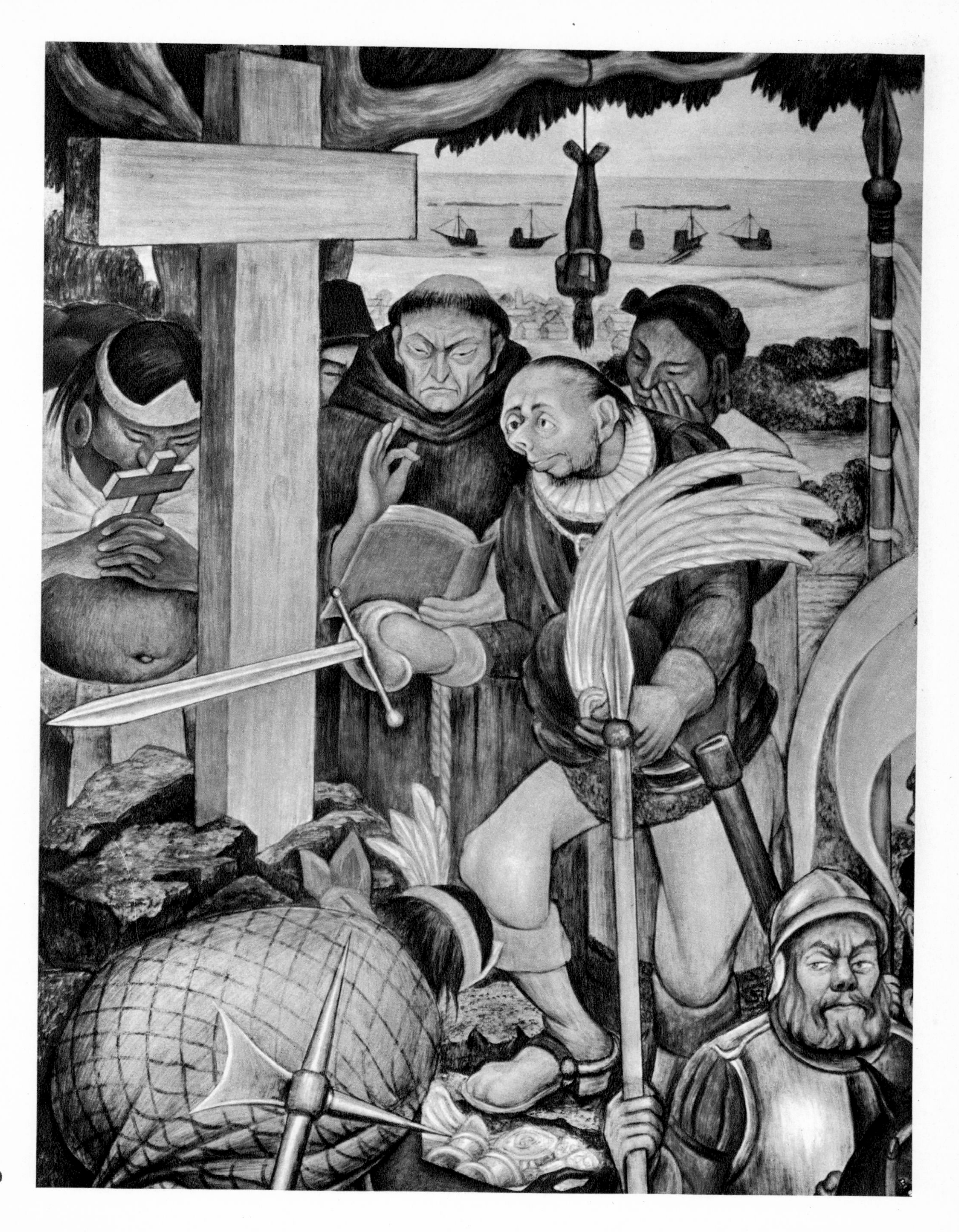

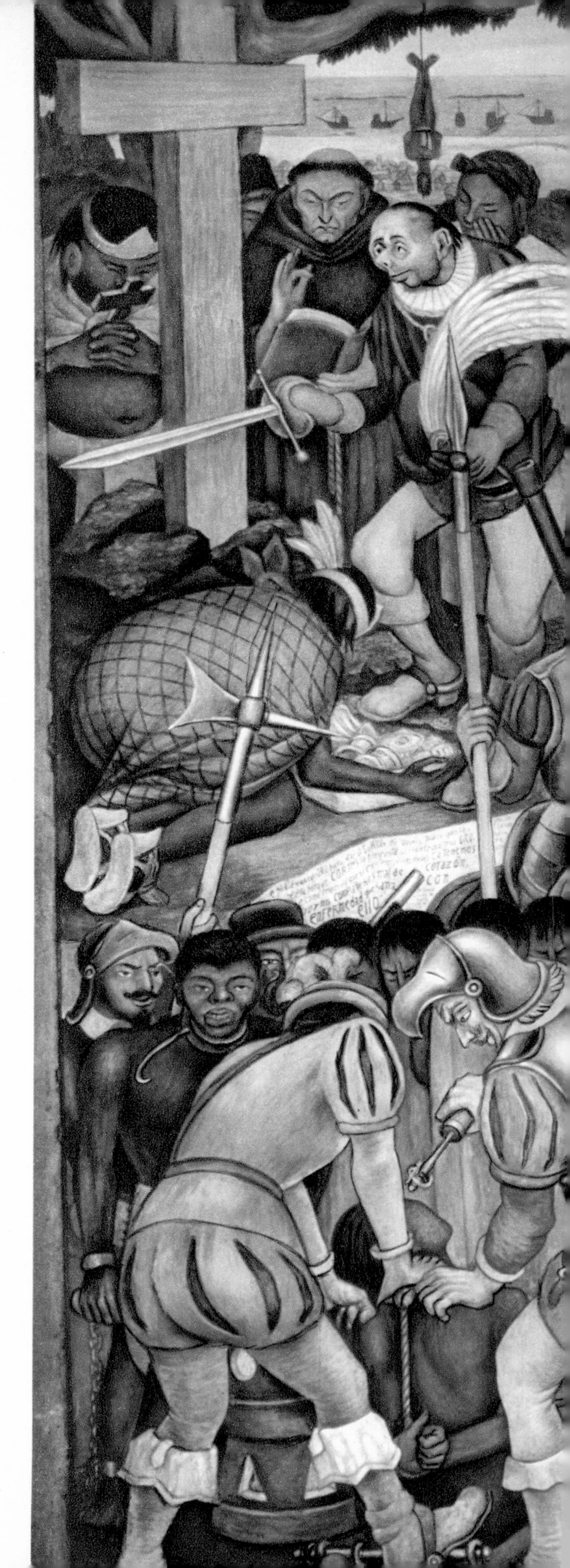

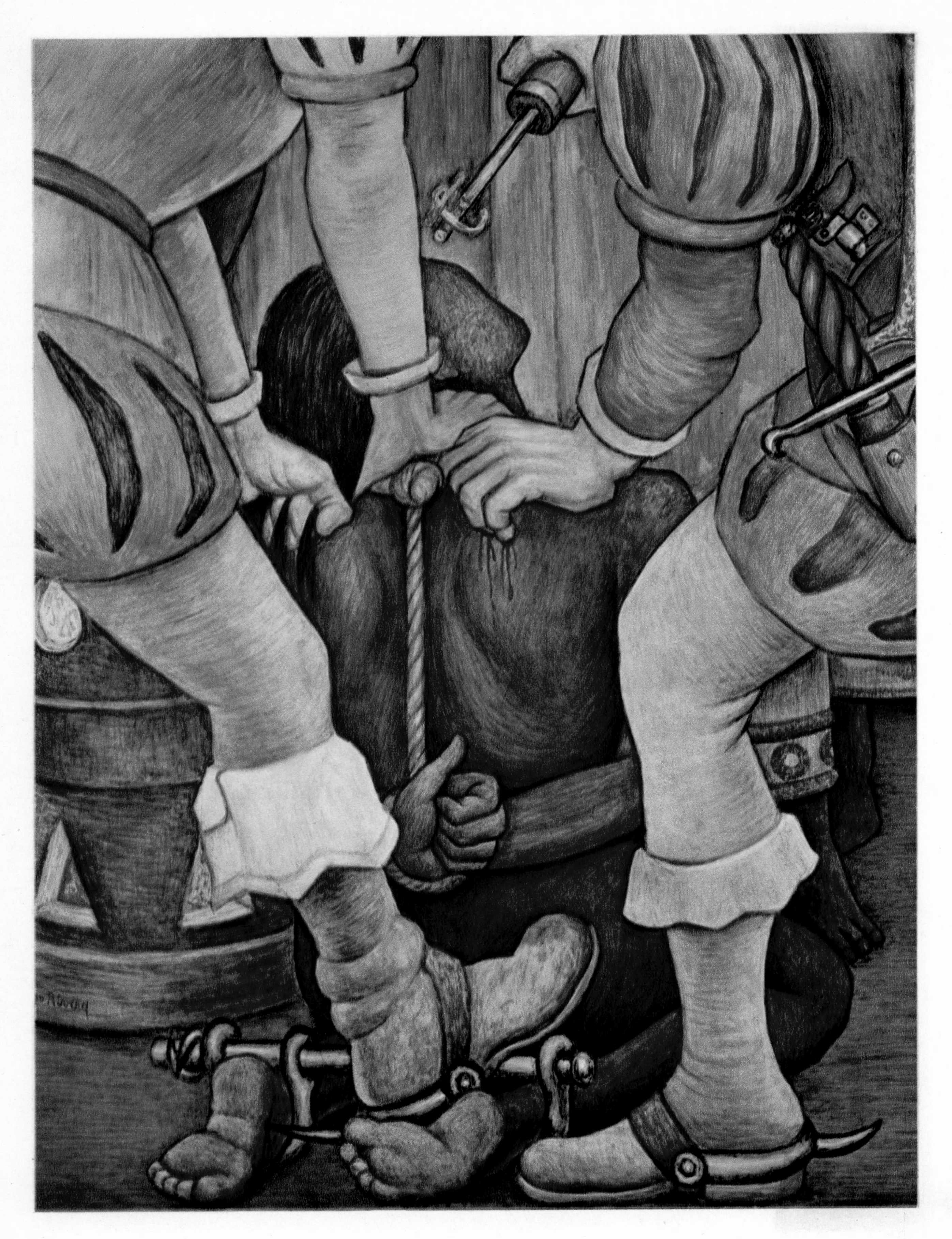

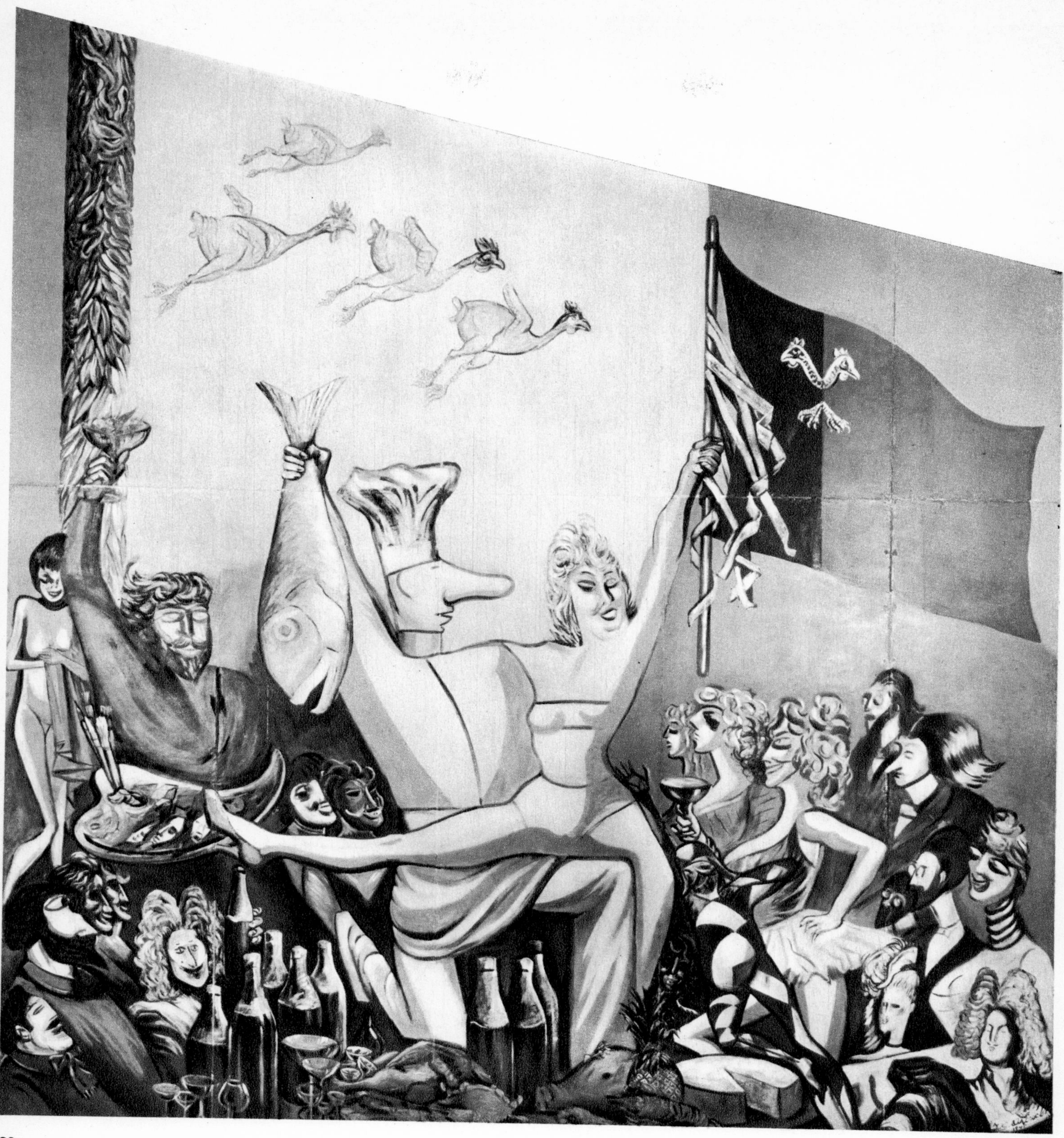

100

101

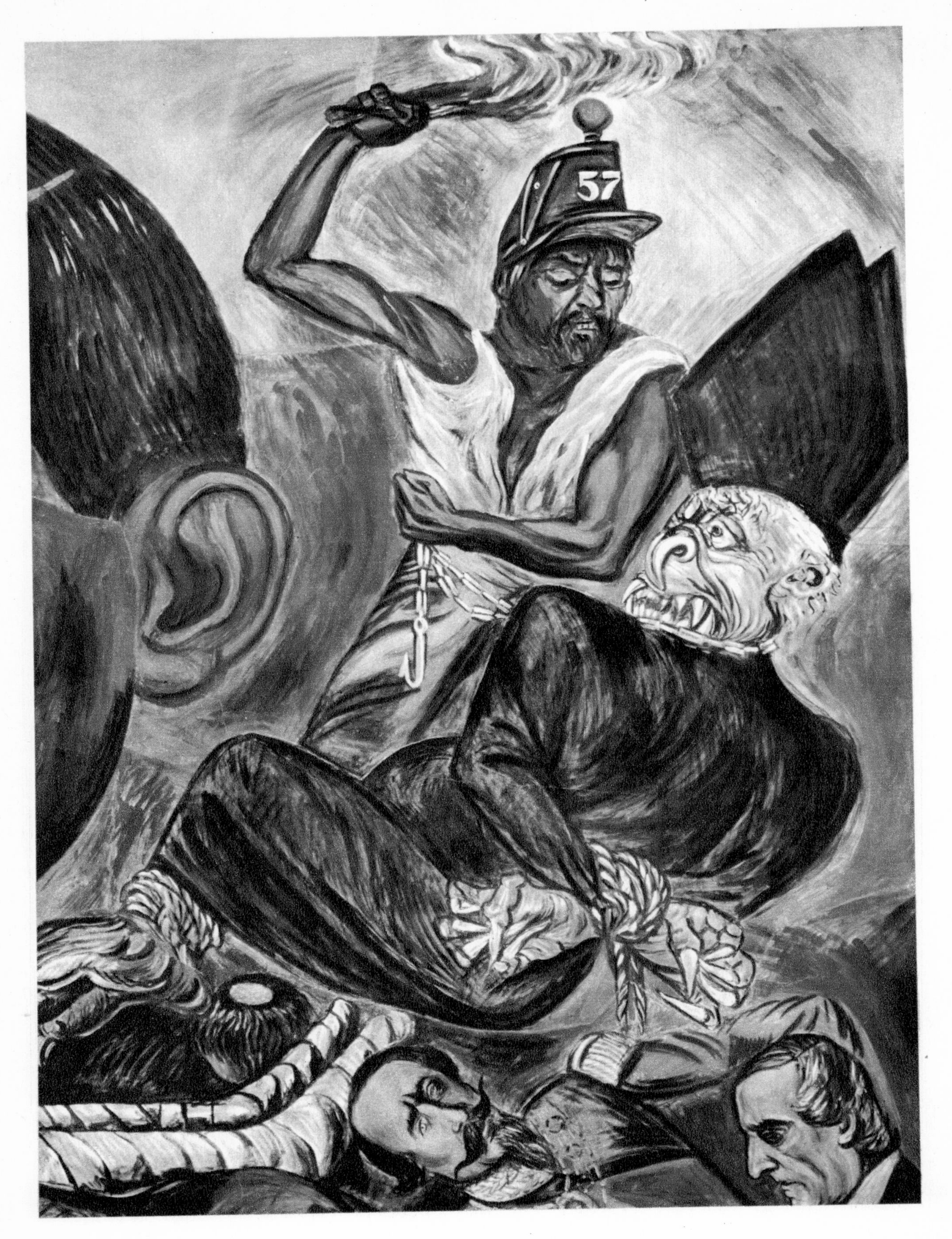
57

BATALLON
SUPREMOS PODERES.
57

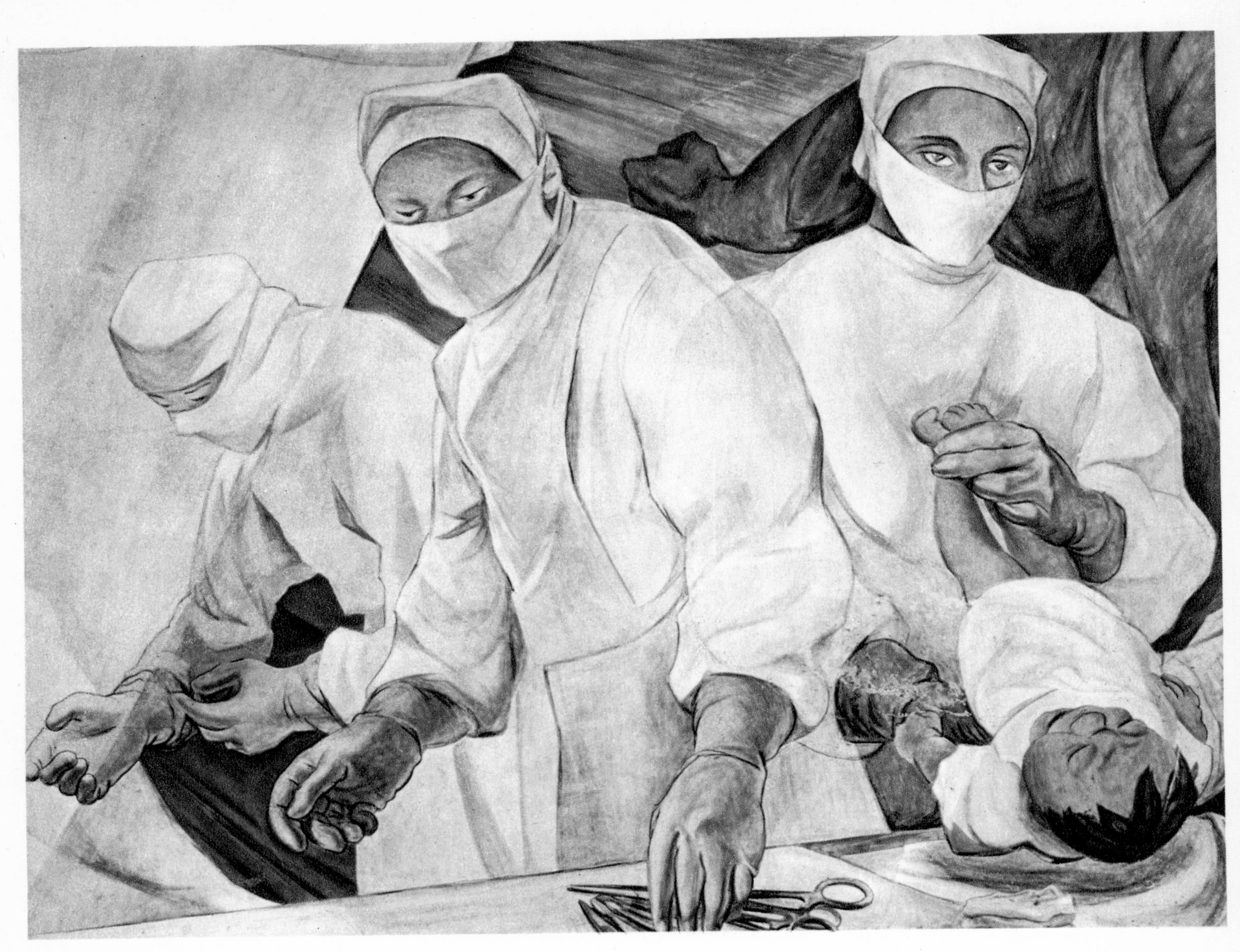

112

113

117

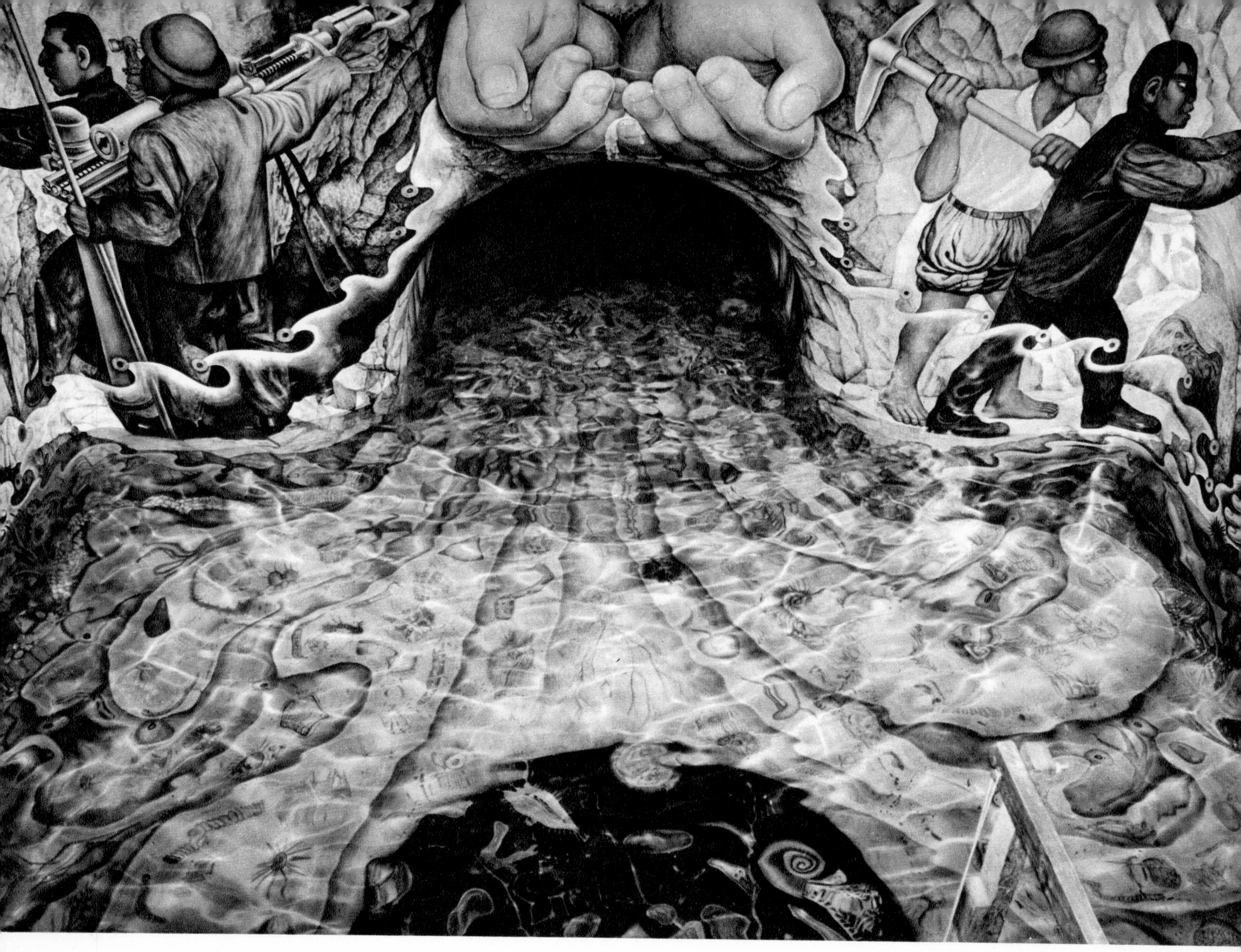

119

120

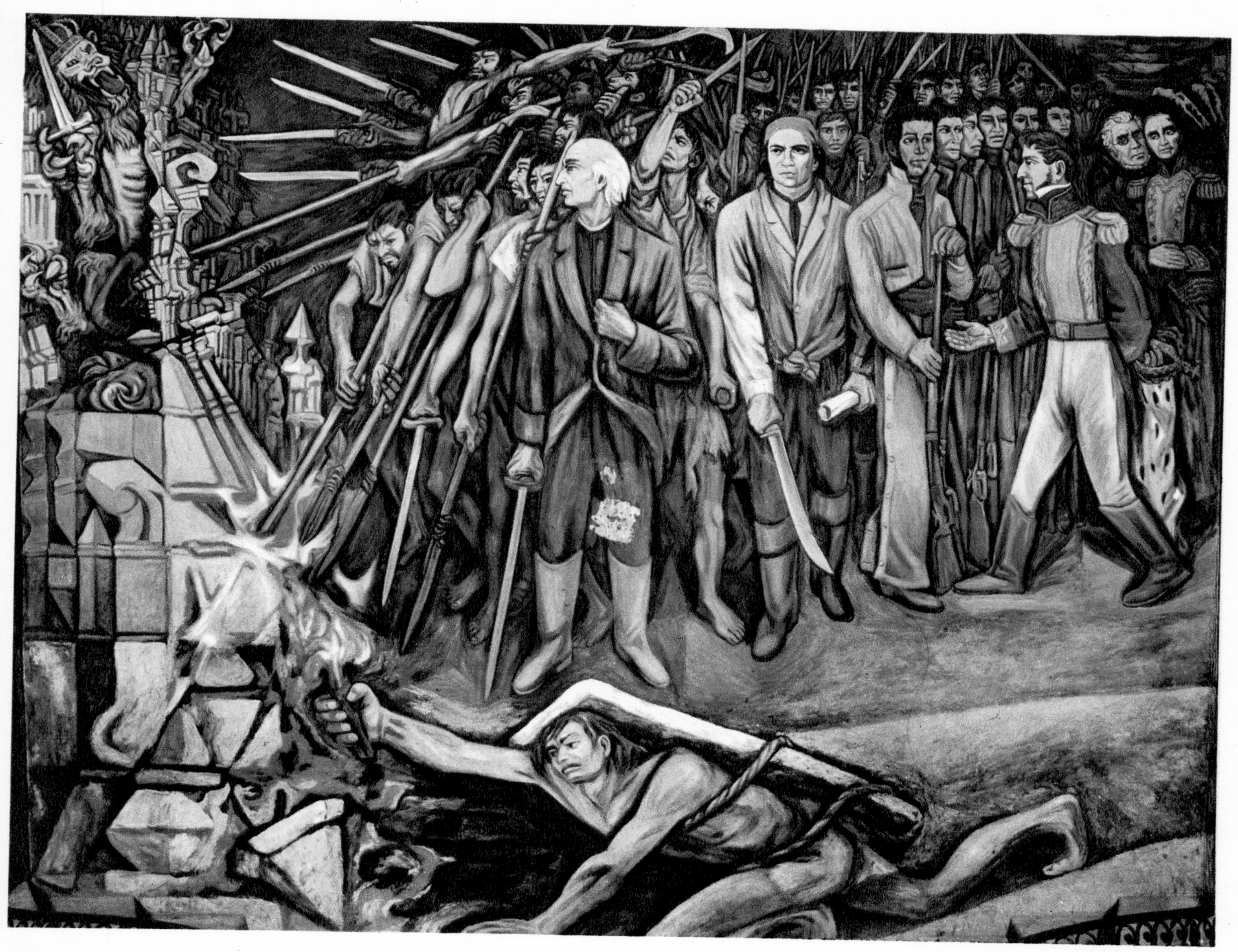

121

123

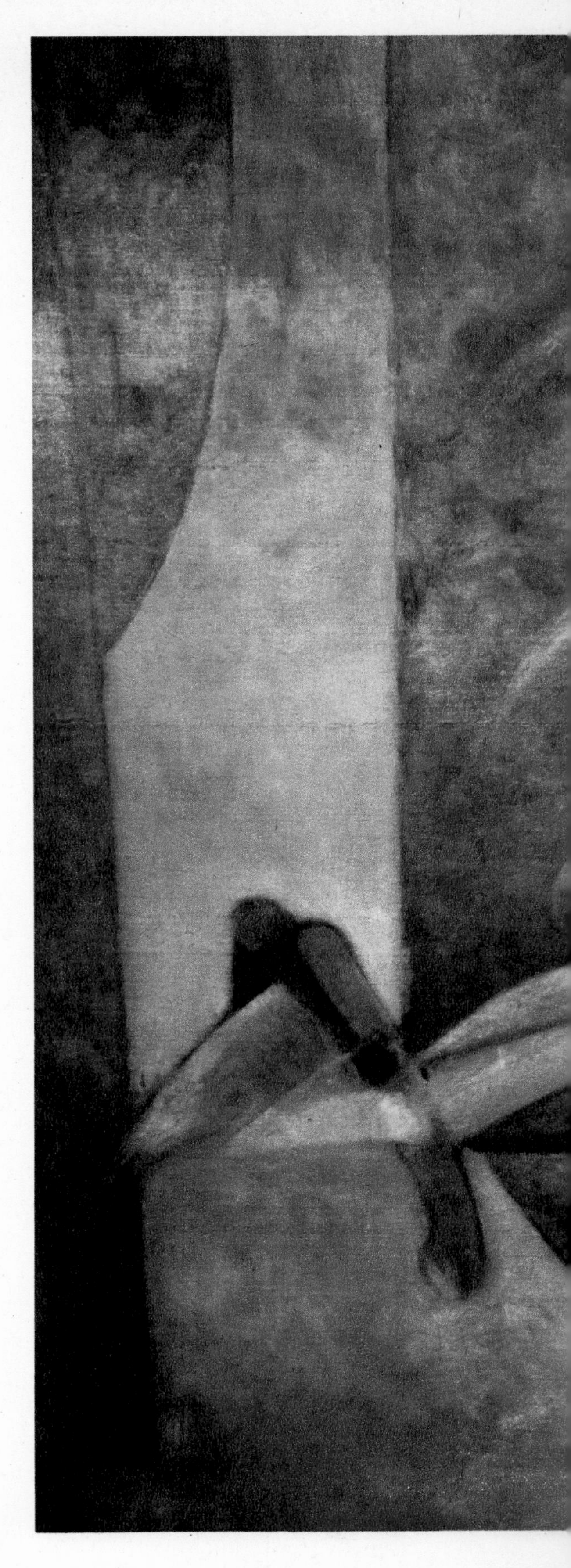

CHAVEZ
MORADO
1955.

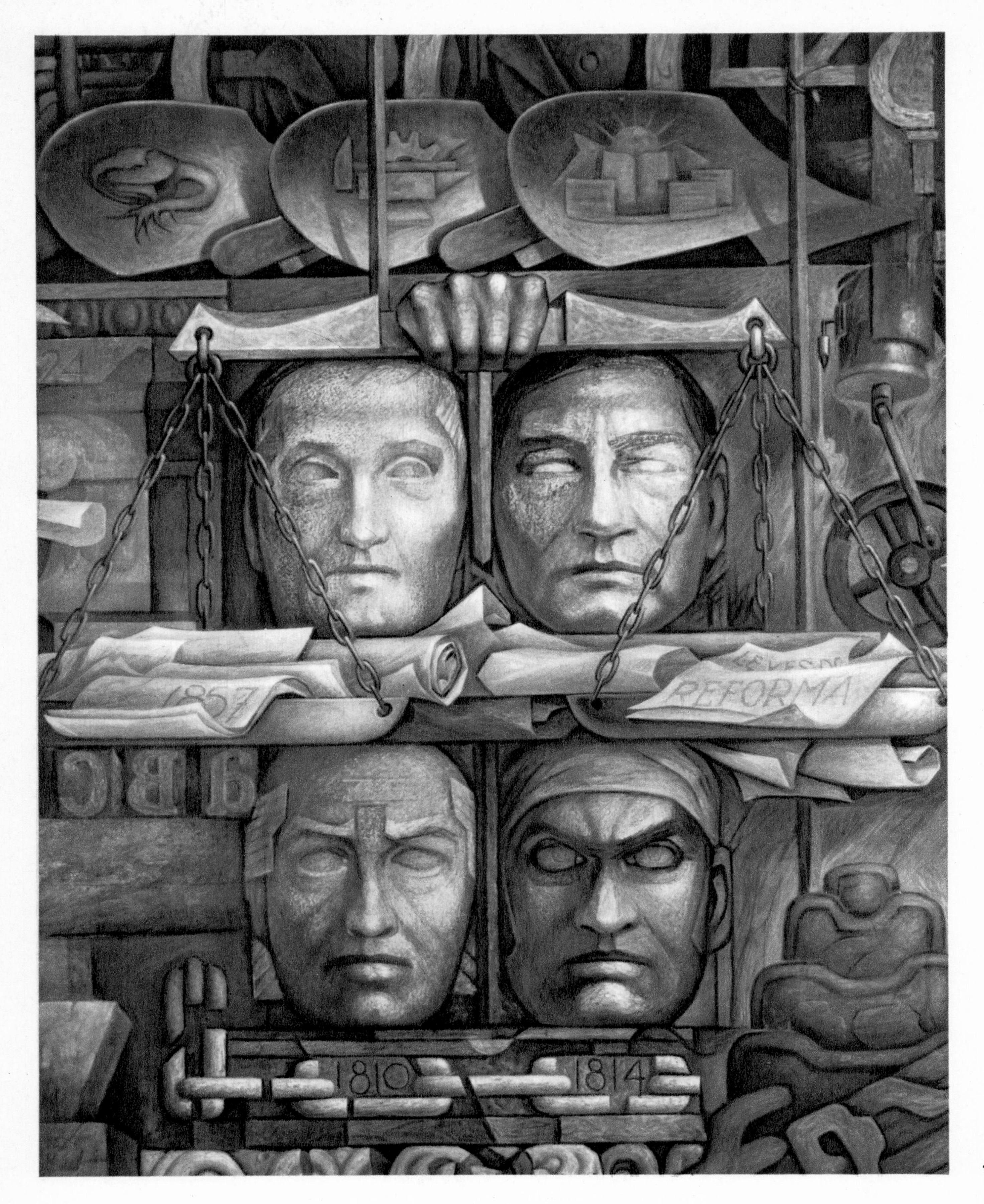
1857
REFORMA
1810
1814

SEGURO
SOCIAL

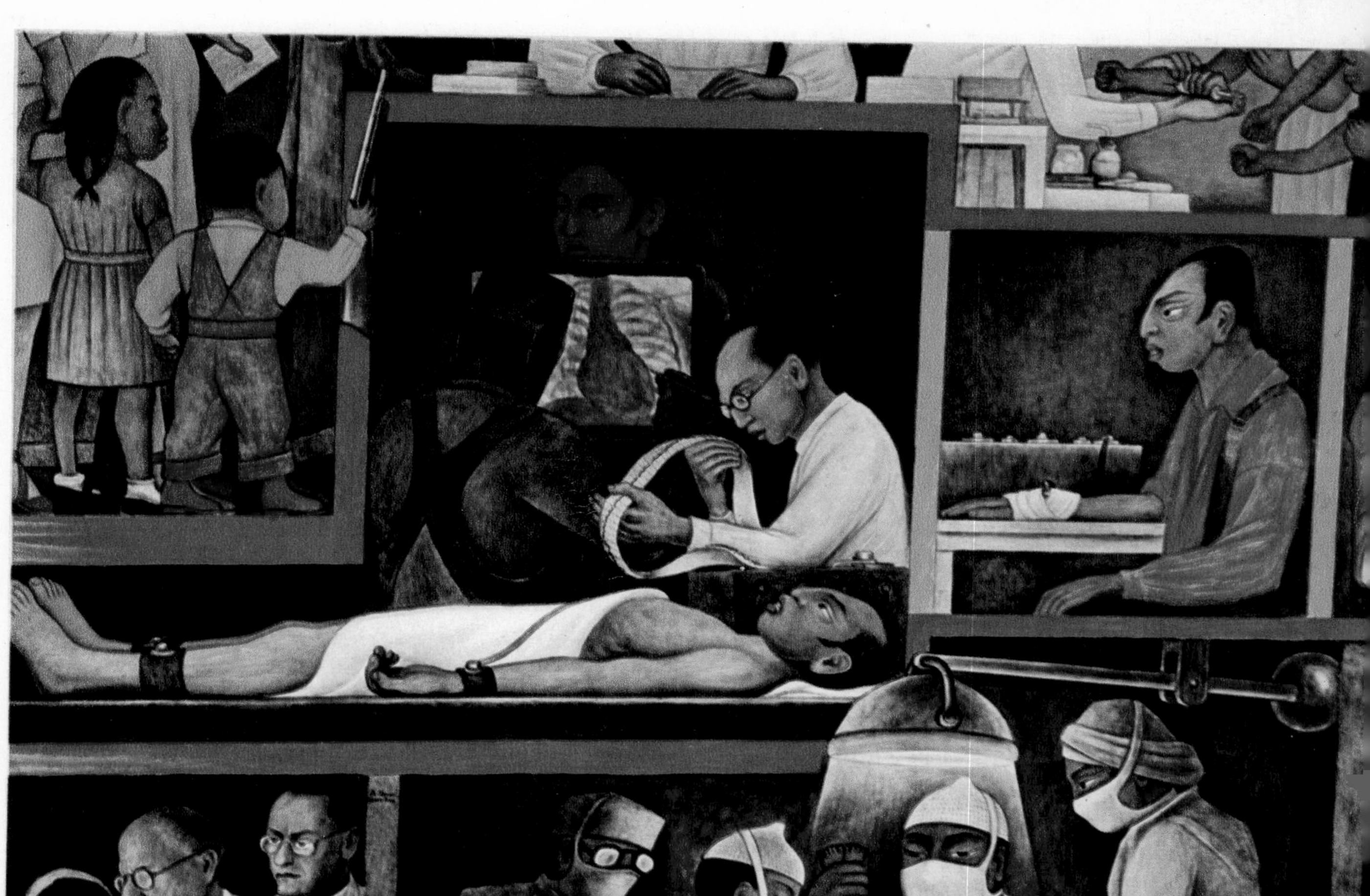

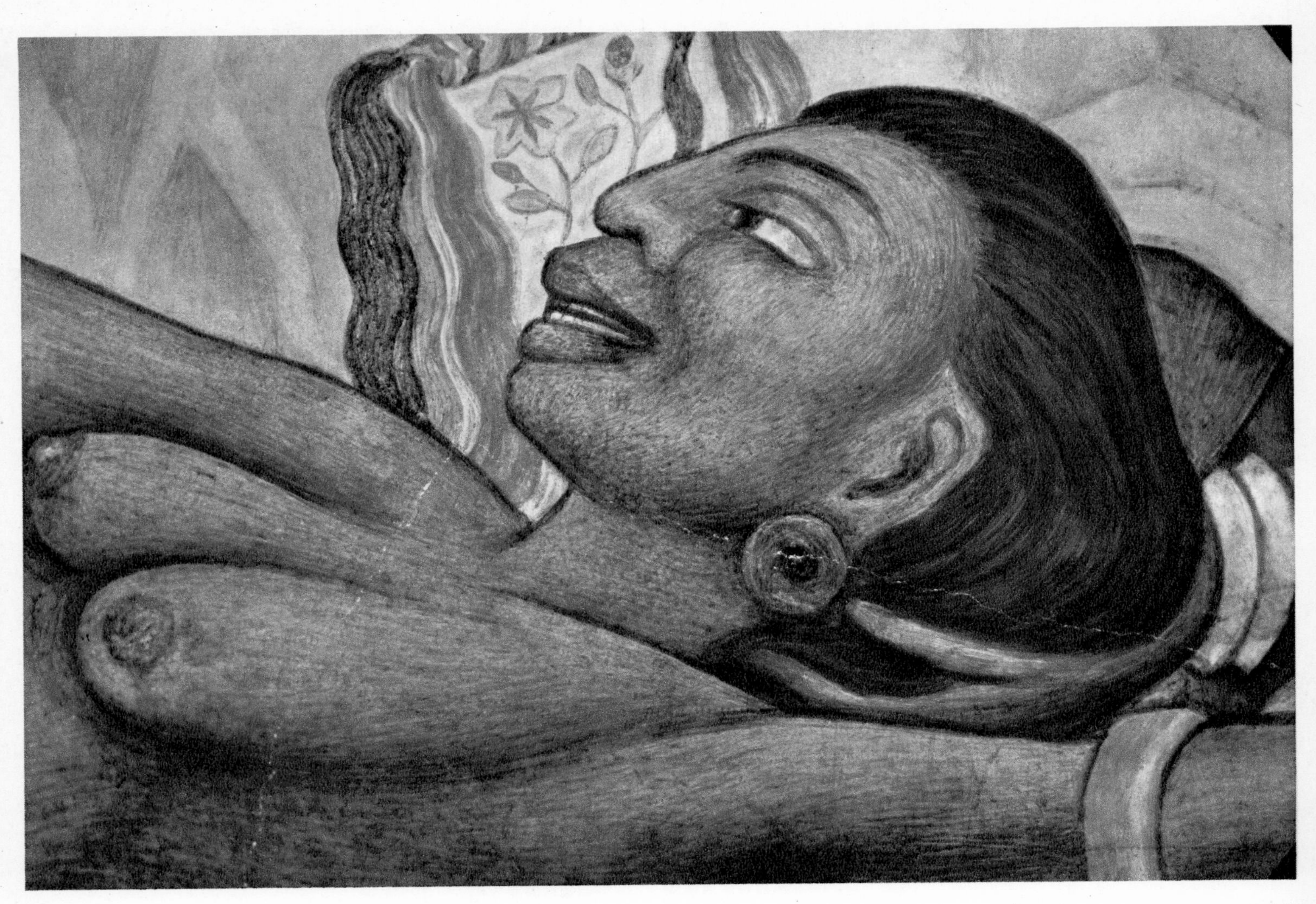

140

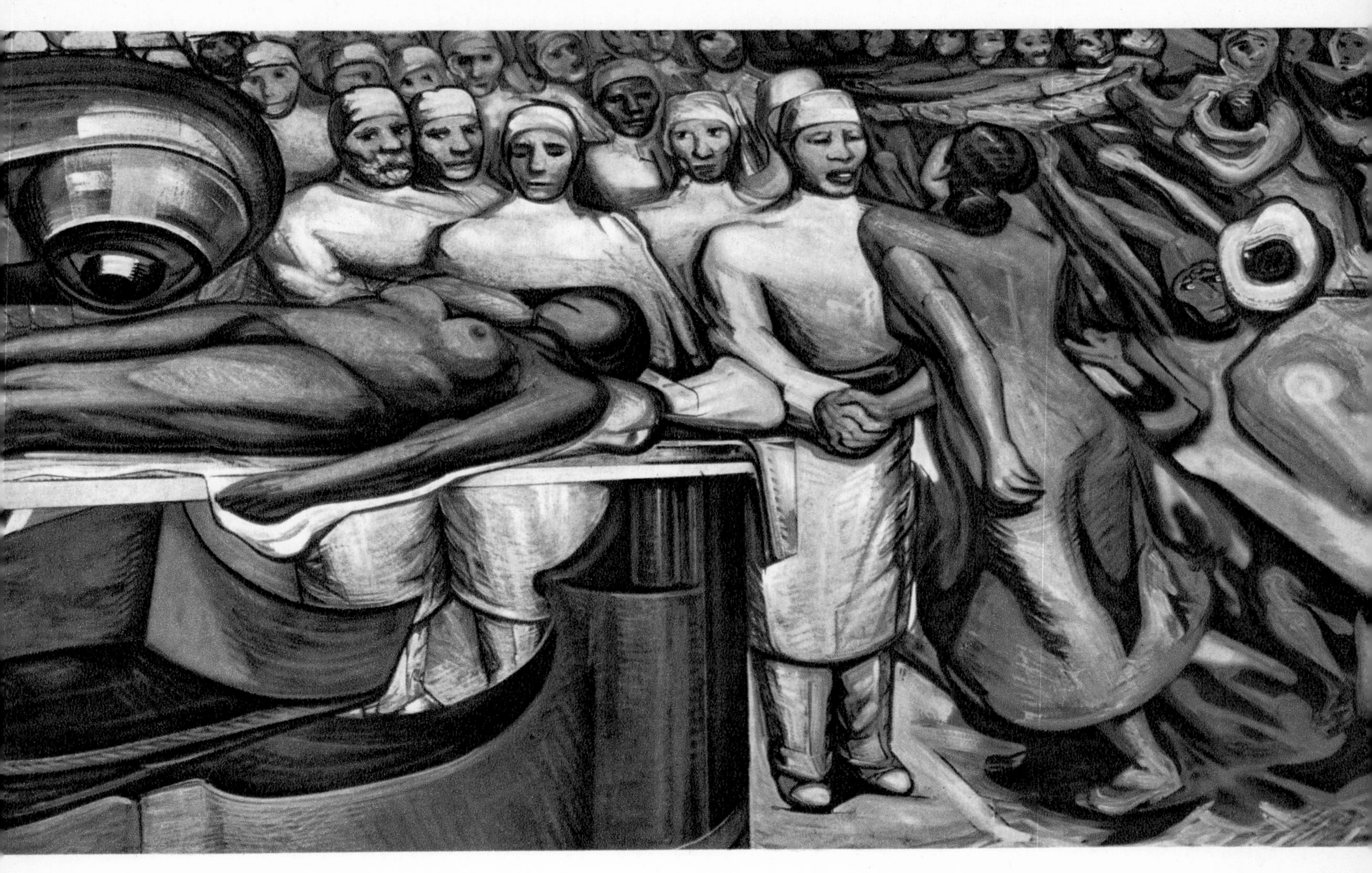

141

145

146

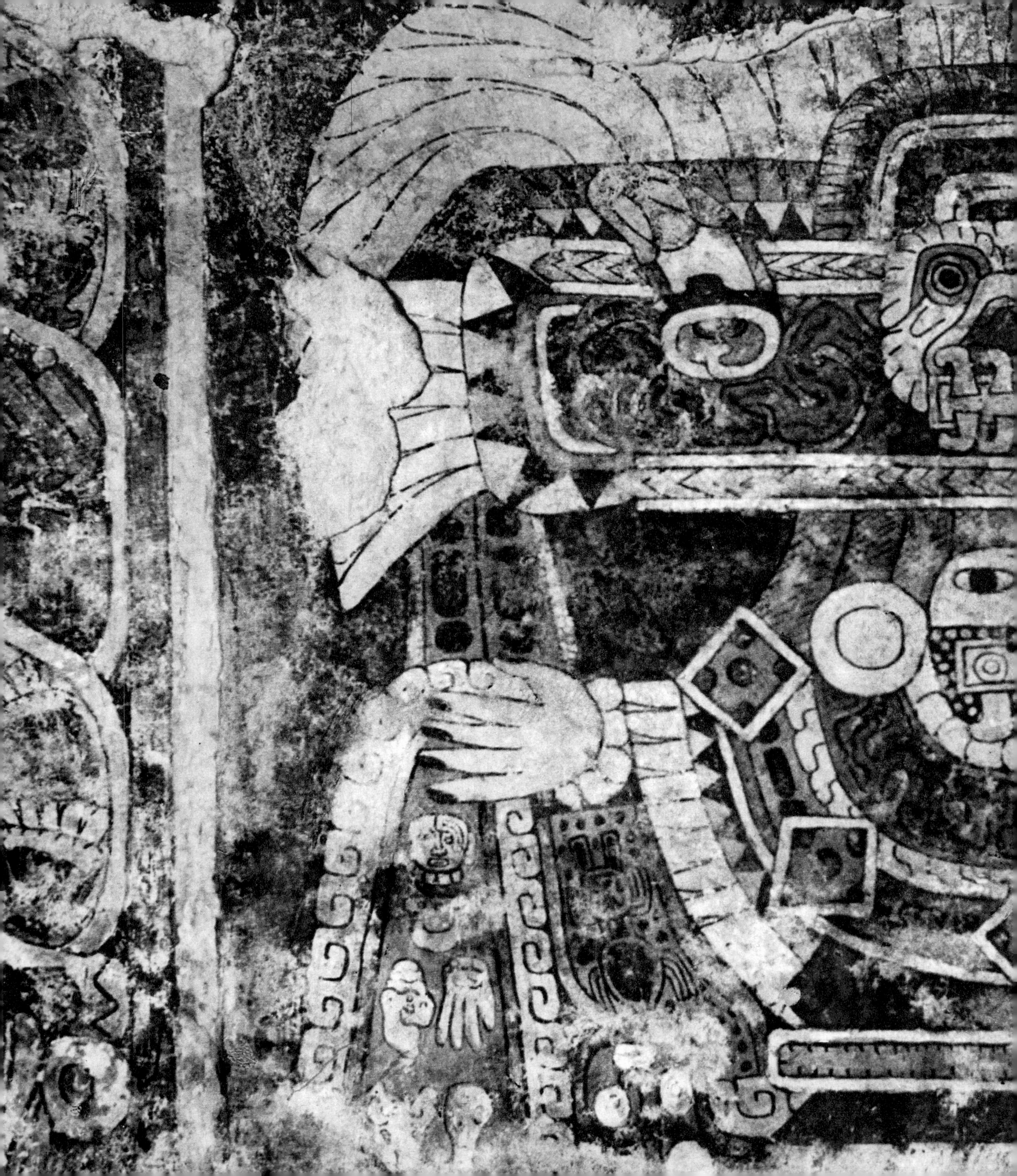